The Christian Witness in a Secular Age

The Christian Witness in a Secular Age

AN EVALUATION OF NINE CONTEMPORARY THEOLOGIANS

By Donald G. Bloesch

Augsburg Publishing House
Minneapolis, Minnesota

THE CHRISTIAN WITNESS IN A SECULAR AGE

Library of Congress Catalog Card No. 68-25803

MANUFACTURED IN THE UNITED STATES OF AMERICA

TO MY PARENTS

IN LOVING APPRECIATION

Acknowledgments

I wish to thank Dr. Theodor Jensen of Wartburg Seminary for his careful reading of this manuscript and also for his very helpful suggestions. A word of appreciation should also be given to *The Dubuque Seminary Journal* for permission to restate part of Chapter X. Finally I wish to express my thanks to my wife for her painstaking reading of this book and for her encouragement.

Foreword

The church today finds itself in a new theological climate. The most pressing theological issue is no longer the two natures of Christ but the relation of Christ to culture; it is not the *real presence* of Christ in the sacrament but the *real difference* between the church and the world. The Christian mission is no longer understood even by such thinkers as Karl Barth and Reinhold Niebuhr as the safeguarding of the purity of the church. Rather it is said that the church should be *in* the world and *for* the world, serving the family of men for whom Christ died. Evangelism is being reinterpreted to mean social outreach and political action. The apologetic task now involves demonstrating the secular relevance of Christian faith rather than proving the authority of the Bible or the existence of God.

This change in theological climate is occasioned by the increasing secularization of modern life. It may be too extreme to assert that God is dead, but we can certainly speak of the demise of institutional religion in the modern world and of the general dissipation of traditional forms of faith. In Europe there is an increasing indifference to the Christian message and a decreasing participation in services of worship. In America there is an increasing indifference to the claims of Christianity accompanied by a continuing but slightly diminishing participation in religious activities. In Europe secularism takes the form of agnosticism and atheism; in America it expresses itself in religiosity or culture religion.

The rise of secularism has brought about a marked change in apologetic theology. In an age in which the very concept of God has become meaningless to vast numbers of people it makes no sense to try to prove his existence. Theologians are now concerning themselves with showing secular man how the Christian faith alleviates the problems of a mass culture and meets genuinely human needs. It is no longer the Christian religion but the law of love and the humanity of Jesus that occupy the attention of apologists.

Hand in hand with this emergence of a new apologetics is a general questioning of the validity of apologetics itself. Indeed some theologians are speaking of the crisis of apologetics just as they had once referred to the crisis of religion. The rise of secularism has cast a shadow over the old apologetics, but has it not also called the very discipline of apologetics into question? The breakdown of confidence in the autonomy of reason and the widespread dominance of relativism in modern culture have made the apologetic task ever more difficult. Post-apologetic theologians, such as Dietrich Bonhoeffer and Karl Barth, maintain that the church today should seek not to make the Gospel relevant to the culture but rather to bring the culture under the scrutiny of the Gospel. I believe that these men are thinking in the right direction.

I concur with many of the secular theologians in saying that the mission of the church is to serve the world. But at the same time is it not also the church's task to call the world to repentance? Indeed, is not this its highest service to the world? We would do well to recognize that although the church should be fundamentally for the world, the world will always be against the church. We agree with both neo-orthodox and secular theologians that there is a pressing need to distinguish between the religion of Christians and the Christian revelation; an urgent need today is to explode the idolatrous culture of our age. Our task is to exorcise the demons which have sought to fill the metaphysical vacuum of modern culture. Is not secularism itself one of these demons?

The new apologetic theologians are right when they contend

that the Gospel must be put in the idiom of modern men, but they are wrong when they seek to abandon the mythical imagery of the Bible. They are right when they try to make the Gospel intelligible and comprehensible to modern culture, but they go astray in their efforts to make it convincing and appealing to the cultured despisers of the faith.

My position is that the Gospel can be known and believed only through its own power. Surely we should acknowledge the poverty of our attempts to prove the superiority of the Gospel over cultural ideologies. The Gospel is not an ideology that can be measured against other ideologies; it is none other than the revealed Word of God that brings all ideologies and religions under divine judgment.

In opposition to popular or culture religion, I maintain that the minister of the Gospel is to be neither a salesman nor a showman, but rather a spokesman for Christ. He is not to depend upon special techniques or strategies of communication; rather he is simply to present the Word of God to his hearers in all its power and clarity. Yet this is an exceedingly difficult assignment; apart from the grace of God it would prove to be impossible to fulfill.

In this time of crisis there are many voices pointing to the road which the church should take if it is to maintain itself in a secular age. Some theologians speak of the need for revival; others emphasize renewal. My view is that what is most needed is a reformation of the church, a reformation which will involve doctrinal restatement as well as new forms of witness and service. Yet there can be no public reformation apart from personal transformation, just as there can be no new forms of church life apart from new men. This is why an authentic reformation must grow out of personal confrontation with the Word of God in Scripture.

What I have attempted to do in this book is to introduce the reader to the contemporary discussion concerning the need to restate the Christian witness in the face of the widespread secularization of modern culture. I have examined in a critical fashion the thought of several important contemporary theologians. In the last chapter I have tried to point to the path which the church should follow if it is to remain true to her mission to bring all men to a saving knowledge of our Lord Jesus Christ.

Contents

Imagine a fortress, absolutely impregnable, provisioned for an eternity.

There comes a new commandment. He conceives that it might be a good idea to build bridges over the moats—so as to be able to attack the besiegers. *Charmant!* He transforms the fortress into a countryseat, and naturally the enemy takes it.

So it is with Christianity. They changed the method —and naturally the world conquered.

SØREN KIERKEGAARD

I.
Introduction: The Secularization of Western Culture

The phenomenon of secularization has compelled Christian theologians today to rethink the message of the faith and to explore new ways by which it can be made intelligible to the post-modern age.[1] The present climate has its immediate roots in the disillusionment associated with the aftermath of the first world war and the worldwide depression in the twenties. Secularization can be defined as a preoccupation with the things of this world and the consequent loss of an ultimate concern. It opens the doorway to secularism, an absolutizing of any relative value or symbol.

That contemporary man and his culture are secularized cannot be gainsaid. Some theologians are now referring to our age as "post-Christian" and even "post-religious." [2] That the advent of secularization has tremendous implications for the apologetic and missionary task of the church must certainly be acknowledged.

In this brief chapter it would be impossible to trace the full development of the secularization of western culture. Yet I shall try to pinpoint the salient features of this secularizing process so that we may be better able to understand the contemporary theological discussion.

It has been customary to view the secularization of the modern world against the background of the ages of faith; this approach, though, must be treated with caution. In the first place, it tends to overlook the accommodation of medieval scholastic theology to pagan classical philosophy. It also does not take into account the superstition and incipient idolatry which characterized much of the popular piety of medieval Christendom. Already among the church fathers there was an attempt motivated partly by an apologetic concern to synthesize Christian faith and Greek philosophy. The early church rejected Gnosticism, the culture Christianity of the first centuries, but in the process it nevertheless arrived at a rapprochement with Greek classical culture.[3] By holding up Christian faith as the highest philosophy the early apologists (such as Justin Martyr, Tatian, and Tertullian) laid the foundation for the conversion of Christianity into a "revealed doctrine." [4]

Yet the church was able to retain its evangelical constitution chiefly because some influential theologians fought the trend toward syncretism. In the West Irenaeus was the principal defender of confessional biblical theology. He was especially vehement against those who contended that the apostles "did . . . frame their doctrine according to the capacity of their hearers, and gave answers after the opinions of their questioners . . . ." [5] Tertullian also at times inveighed against syncretistic theology, but his own approach was basically apologetic. His hostility to syncretism can be seen in his *On Prescription Against Heretics* where he asks: "What indeed has Athens to do with Jerusalem? What concord is there between the Academy and the Church? What between heretics and Christians?" [6] In the East, Athanasius was among those who held fast to the apostolic faith. He sought to capture and transform the speculation of his day, but he never succumbed to it.[7] Augustine was also a brilliant defender of the faith against pagan culture and philosophy, although at least the beginnings of a synthesis with classical culture can be seen in his thought. In Thomas Aquinas and the later scholastics this synthesis was very much established; nevertheless the fundamentals of the faith were preserved, even though somewhat concealed in a philosophical framework. Despite the vigorous apologetic efforts of Augustine, Aquinas, and the later scholastics, it cannot be denied that in their theologies the dynamic biblical orientation of the faith was partly subverted.[8]

The lay religious orders and brotherhoods comprised one of the chief sources of renewal in the medieval church. Despite the tendency toward works-righteousness which was present in many of these groups, the radical claims of biblical faith were recovered at least for a time. Even the biblical message of free grace frequently made itself heard among the itinerant evangelists, friars, and monks. Bernard of Clairvaux, the great Cistercian preacher, and Thomas à Kempis, a member of the Brethren of the Common Life, were among those who reaffirmed the doctrine of salvation by the grace of God alone. The religious orders and communities represented sources of new life at the beginning of their histories, but when they became institutionalized they frequently lost their charismatic and revolutionary character and became as moribund as the church itself.

Despite the intellectual compromises it made with secular or pagan thought, the culture of medieval Europe was still permeated with Christian values and concern. This culture cannot be regarded as "Christian" in the sense that men had attained a brotherhood of love under the lordship of Christ, nor can it be considered Christian in the sense that the church was proclaiming the evangelical message in its complete purity; yet faith in a transcendent and living God was almost universally prevalent. Even those who did not accept the Gospel and who rebelled against the authority of the church still acknowledged the existence of a supernatural God and also of a heavenly world beyond this world. Medieval culture was beset by periods of retrogression, but these were always counterbalanced by periods of renewal.

At the same time, as the medieval church became more established and scholastic philosophy flourished, the seeds of decay were already beginning to germinate. Despite the general heavenward and Godward orientation of this culture, heteronomy (the centering of authority in an external standard or institution) tended more and more to replace theonomy (the grounding of authority in God). Augustine anticipated the movement toward heteronomy when he said: "I should not believe the Gospel except as moved by the authority of the Catholic Church." By the late Middle Ages, the symbols of the faith had hardened into inflexible standards and rigid dogmas.

The post-medieval period (14th to 16th centuries) marks a transition from the Middle Ages to the modern age. Here can be seen the flowering of the Renaissance which signalized a movement away from heteronomy to autonomy (authority centered in the self), but this was an autonomy still open to God. The freedom and dignity of man were emphasized, but this was still understood as a freedom under God. The crass opportunism of Machiavelli was not characteristic of this period. The Renaissance was in part a reaction to a rigid heteronomy in which the institutional church and its creeds seemed to supplant the authority of the living God.

The Renaissance emphases augured the breakup of the biblical-classical synthesis which characterized medieval scholastic theology. Nominalism and mysticism supplanted the older scholastic philosophy. Nominalism cast doubt upon the sufficiency of reason alone to confirm the existence of God and the authority of the biblical revelation. The only reality open to reason was said to be that of the world of particulars or things, the world accessible to sense perception.

Mysticism reached its apogee in the 14th century. The mystics (such as Eckhart, Suso, and Tauler) sought to reaffirm the necessity of a direct relationship with the living God, but mysticism also pointed in the direction of autonomy. It was not the sacraments nor the voice of the church but the inward voice or light of God that was considered to be the ground of certainty. Yet this inner light was never divorced from the Spirit of God, nor did this mysticism (with one or two exceptions) obscure or deny the qualitative difference between God and man.

The Protestant Reformation of the 16th century brought about a partial restoration of theocentric biblical faith. Luther and Calvin protested against the biblical-classical synthesis, which they regarded as a distortion of evangelical truth. The criterion for faith, they contended, is not natural reason but the revelation of Jesus Christ as witnessed to and conveyed in Holy Scripture. For the Reformers the truth of faith cannot be defended at the bar of natural reason, but it can and must be explicated by a reborn reason. In their theology salvation consists not in the mystical ascent to perfection but rather in the forgiveness of sins and the new life in Jesus Christ. The locus of the Holy is not primarily the institutional church or the sacraments but the living Christ who stands in judgment over all human culture and religion. The Catholic Counter-Reformation came into being to meet the Protestant challenge; at the same time it also sought to call the church back to its spiritual foundations. The message of *sola gratia* and *sola fide* found new expression in the writings of such mystics as John of the Cross and Teresa of Avila.

Yet the Reformation was not an unqualified success, since in the process the Evangelical and Roman wings of the Catholic Church were divided. The children of both the Reformation and the Counter-Reformation were placed on the defensive not only against one another but also against the rising tide of humanism. Despite the momentary restoration of theonomy in the first part of the 16th century, the lapse into heteronomy soon followed. In Protestantism the Bible as an objective standard was invested with absolute value. Faith once again came to be defined in terms of intellectual assent *(credentia)* as over against heartfelt trust *(fiducia).* In Roman Catholicism authority was placed more and more in the papal office. Two sources of revelation were propounded by Catholic theologians—Scripture and tradition—and the church thereby became exempt from searching self-criticism. The Reformation, then, was a tragedy as well as a necessity; the central message of the faith was recovered for a time, but the unity of Christendom was perhaps irreparably severed.

The roots of modern secularism can be found in the dissolution of the medieval synthesis. Yet neither the Renaissance nor the Reformation can be held fully responsible, since the medieval church by its arrogance and presumption also helped make the modern secular revolution inevitable. The Renaissance, after all, was a reaction to the attempt by the church to deny the authenticity and relative autonomy of the secular. The church's absolutizing of theological and ecclesiastical forms, sometimes described as sacralization (Barth) and also as demonization (Tillich), can be regarded as just another kind of secularization.

Yet secularism did not come into its own until the Enlightenment (17th and 18th centuries). Freedom of thought became free thought, and autonomy triumphed. This was the age of the self-sufficient and independent individual (like Leibnitz' monads).

Descartes laid the groundwork for Enlightenment philosophy in his phrase: "I think, therefore I am." John Locke, despite his empirical critique of much of the rationalism of his day, also reflected the Enlightenment in his affirmation: "Reason must be our last judge and guide in everything." [9]

The principal kind of religion at this time was Deism, which affirmed the existence of God but denied his creative activity in the world. Christianity was relegated to the realm of personal piety. Attention was focused on the laws of nature and on universal truths. Even in the circles of Protestant orthodoxy natural theology and an idealistic philosophy of religion were prevalent if not dominant. The Christian faith was reduced to certain axioms that were believed to be self-evident to all men.[10]

The idea that reason is capable of proving the existence of God and many other truths of faith permeated both Catholic and Evangelical apologetics. It was not the reconciling action of God in biblical history but the universal idea of God or the design of God in nature that occupied the attention of the apologists. The miracles and biblical prophecy also played a large role in the apologetic enterprise, particularly among the more orthodox theologians. Here again it can be seen that the defenders of the faith compromised the faith by basing their case on the presuppositions of their opponents, that is, on the sole sufficiency of reason and natural law.

It was in the French Revolution toward the end of the 18th century that Enlightenment philosophy crystallized into the worship of Reason. In France the first secular state in the modern sense came into being, although it could not maintain itself for long. Libations were poured out to statues of Nature; political heroes instead of saints were the objects of veneration; goddesses of Reason replaced statues of the Virgin in Catholic churches in Paris and in countless village churches; clergymen and members of religious orders were forbidden to teach in the public schools, and salaries for clergymen were discontinued. The cult of Reason reached its climax in Robespierre's celebration of Reason's Festival of the Supreme Being on June 8, 1794. For all practical purposes, Christianity was emasculated.

Pietism and Evangelicalism were movements that reacted against the Enlightenment and thereby blunted the force of rationalistic religion. Yet by turning attention to inner piety, these movements were unable to stem the tide toward subjectivism and relativism. By placing the accent on personal salvation they even reflected the Enlightenment motif of individualism. This, however, is not to deny the fact that they preserved a theonomous orientation in a time when rationalism was dominant. It can be said that the Second Great Awakening in early 19th century America saved that nation from rationalistic humanism and Deism, which were rampant in the American Revolution.

The Romanticism of the later 18th and 19th centuries brought reason itself into question. The emergence of the Romantic movement should be viewed as a reaction against both the rationalism of the Enlightenment and the mechanistic materialism which the Enlightenment encouraged in its later stages. The Romanticists challenged the doctrine that we arrive at truth by means of "clear and distinct ideas." It is not by abstract reasoning, they argued, but through feeling and experience that we confront reality. The only valid epistemological criterion is not a universal or divine reason but rather intuition or mystical insight. It was not long before the universality of natural law was called into question. Just as the Enlightenment had subverted the idea of a historical revelation, so now Romanticism relativized the ethic which cannot long sustain itself apart from that revelation.

Both philosophy and theology were soon caught up in this new mood, which eventually resulted in the enthronement of the feelings and drives of men. Immanuel Kant, although basically a child of the Enlightenment, helped to prepare the way for Romanticism by asserting in his *Critique of Pure Reason* that reason itself cannot penetrate ultimate reality. In his *Critique of Judgment* he suggested that moral and aesthetic intuition can bring us into contact with ultimate reality even though they cannot render determinative knowledge. Hegel's philosophy signified a reaction against Romanticism in favor of the Enlightenment, and yet even Hegel held that reason has a "fate," that is to say, is conditioned. Marx spoke of the ideological taint in human reasoning. Freud and Nietzsche also pointed to the limitations and conditioning of man's reasoning; they affirmed that man is motivated chiefly by inner drives and passions. Nietzsche even proclaimed the "death of God," now a major theme in contemporary theology. The English poet Swinburne echoed the buoyant and sometimes arrogant optimism of the later Romantic period when he wrote: "Glory to man in the highest; he is the measure of all things."

Through its emphasis on individuality and particularity, Romanticism paved the way for nationalism and racism. The doctrine of the sovereignty of the people or race began to supplant the biblical affirmation of the sovereignty of God. The early Romanticists were fervent patriots—some of them were even intransigent nationalists—but they did not yet deify the national or racial corpus. It was only in the first decades of the 20th century that the nationalism of the early Romanticists, Carlyle's hero worship, Gobineau's racism, and Nietzsche's will to power ethic were joined into a vitriolic religion. Only then did the subtle relationship between Romanticism and modern fascism become evident.

Friedrich Schleiermacher (1768-1834) set the pattern for modern theology in his attempt to mediate between Christian faith and Romanticism. In his *Addresses to the Cultured Despisers of Religion* he sought to vindicate not the Christian faith itself so much as religion in general. He succumbed to the very relativism which he attacked when he asserted that men apprehend the Infinite in different ways and that consequently there is no one form of religion that is absolute for men. Although he held that Christianity is the highest of the religions, he saw a time when the faith of the church would be supplanted by new and more vital religions.

In his monumental *The Christian Faith* Schleiermacher defined faith as a feeling of absolute dependence, which in his view is the basic reaction of men to God. He took pains to point out that although this feeling is universal, the Christian is most aware of it. Christianity differs from other religions, therefore, only in degree and not in kind. On the whole, pantheistic motifs dominate much of his theological speculation. God is thought of as being continuous with nature; sin is the dominance of the lower nature within us rather than a radical perversion of our essential nature; reconciliation is conceived in terms of a process in the human soul rather than a divine intervention in history.

Schleiermacher, to be fair, was an earnest Christian thinker who sought to reconcile the claims of biblical faith with the *Zeitgeist* (spirit of the times). Moreover, he recovered certain dimensions of the faith which had been neglected in the older orthodoxy, such as the necessity for the response of faith and the cultivation of the inner life. At the same time, by seeking to make religion palatable to its cultured despisers, he compromised certain basic Christian truths. He thereby contributed to the dissolution and secularization of the Christian faith in the modern world.

The basic ideology which permeated both the Enlightenment and Romanticist philosophies (and indeed much of 20th century humanism) is the belief in human progress and the redemptive character of history. This ideology was in the process of formation already in the 18th century, but it was given tremendous impetus in the 19th century by the publication in 1859 of Darwin's *Origin of Species,* which propounded the theory of biological evolution. Both secular and Christian thinkers began speculating beyond the limits of Darwin's work; they spoke of the religious and even the moral evolution of the human race. Reinhold Niebuhr has contended that the ideology of progress is the hallmark of the modern age, since it has permeated almost every intellectual discipline including theology.

Kant had anticipated this emphasis in his work *Eternal Peace,* in which he foresaw the possibility of an eternal peace on earth through moral improvement. Auguste Comte, the guiding spirit of French positivism, saw the history of mankind divided into three stages: the theological, the metaphysical, and the positive. We are now at the dawn of the positive age, he contended, in which scientists content themselves with the observation of phenomena, no longer attributing them to a supernatural force or power. Despite his anti-theological bias, Comte perceived the psychological value of religion; he attempted to establish a cult centered about the worship of "Humanity." The German theologian and apologist Albrecht Ritschl reflected the ideology of progress in his conception of the kingdom of God being progressively realized in history. Some of his later followers even spoke of the building of the kingdom of God on earth by eradicating social injustice.

The conservative evangelical sects mirrored the historical optimism of the modern age in their doctrine of the millennium, the thousand-year period when Christ would reign on earth. It must be borne in mind, however, that the sectarian evangelicals regarded the millennial age as being inaugurated by supernatural intervention. Marx's idea of a proletarian utopia as the climax of the historical process is a secularized version of millenarianism.

The two world wars of this century have punctured the optimistic illusions of modern men, but the ideology of progress is still not dead. The idea of the "world come of age" which is to be found in Bonhoeffer, Robinson, and Cox seems to echo this ideology. The apologetics of Teilhard de Chardin, oriented about the idea of creative emergent evolution, also appears to mirror the historical optimism of an earlier period.

In the twentieth century the dominant philosophical moods have been relativism and nihilism. This has been aptly called the century of the death of man (Samuel Beckett). The principal philosophies—existentialism, psychoanalysis, analytic philosophy, process philosophy, and dialectical materialism—all point to the relativism inherent in a totally secular society.[11] Paul Tillich contends that the dominant malady of the present age is the anxiety of meaninglessness. The analytic philosophers are preoccupied with the problem of the meaning of meaning. The erratic symbolism in modern art reflects the desperate attempt on the part of many intellectuals to find purpose in an age of chaos. The preoccupation of modern novelists with abnormality and anxiety points to the breakdown of spiritual forces. In some Iron Curtain nations, the idealism of messianic Communism is degenerating into cynicism and opportunism. Western capitalism is proving to be nothing other than a practical materialism which is unable to satisfy man's search for meaning.

Emil Brunner has wisely averred that the metaphysical dimensions of men's minds cannot remain empty.[12] If man has lost faith in all absolutes, then he will manufacture gods for himself. In this period of relativism and cynicism new secular salvations are emerging. We are witnessing today the recrudescence of the titanic gods of race, nation, hero, and class. Even the ancient gods of fertility and sex are again becoming live options for secularized man. Syncretistic mystical cults are also appearing which further erode the spiritual heritage of western culture.

Contemporary theology has for the most part reflected the despair and relativism of the post-modern age. Ernst Troeltsch in the early part of the century was already stating that Christianity can be regarded as absolute only for western man.[13] According to Bultmann, the Christian can no longer affirm an objective historical resurrection and can speak only of an existential "experience of the cross." In his theology the only God that we can affirm is the beyond in the midst of this world, the unconditional in the conditional.[14] Harvey Cox maintains that a God who totally transcends the world is no longer intelligible to modern man, but that it is possible to speak of God as the moving force behind and within secular political events. Theologians such as Tillich and John Robinson hold that the concept of a supernatural personal God is now passé, that God can be spoken of intelligibly only as the ground of being or the depth of selfhood. The neo-naturalists (Wieman, Ogden, Cobb), in seeking to bring Christian faith into accord with Whitehead's philosophy, see God as a creative process within and limited to the natural order. Thomas Altizer vigorously denies the reality of what he terms the Christian God and speaks instead after the manner of Hegel of a world Spirit realizing itself in humanity. Rabbi Richard Rubenstein contends that belief in the biblical God of history is no longer possible; he advocates a return to the gods of nature and the cycle of natural life.

Neo-orthodox theology, associated with the names of Karl Barth, Reinhold Niebuhr, and Emil Brunner, has sought to stem the drift toward relativism by emphasizing again the uniqueness of Jesus Christ and the authority of the biblical revelation. The lines between the holy God and secular culture were drawn quite sharply in the original theology of crisis, although Barth is now placing the accent on the identification of God with humanity. Barth's view that all men are in Christ whether they realize it or not tends to mitigate the difference between the church and the world. He maintains that all men have been placed in the kingdom of Christ by virtue of the triumph of the resurrection although he will not say that all men are in the covenant community. Yet in his theology the lines between faith and unfaith, church and world are considerably blurred. Reinhold Niebuhr speaks of a hidden Christ who is present wherever men commit themselves to social righteousness. His distinction between the children of light and the children of darkness is made not on the basis of whether men have faith but on whether they have social concern.

Concurrent with the secularization of theology is the secularization of morality. Absolute moral standards are now rejected in most theological circles. In place of an ethics oriented about the law and the Gospel we find situational and contextual ethics. The "new morality" upheld by Robinson, Cox, Fletcher, and others makes love the final criterion for action, but their description of love is not really related in any organic way to the revealed law of God given in the Bible. The secular revolution in sexual mores today is reflected in the theological revolt against a morality of authority. When the reality of a transcendent God is doubted, the "good" is also called into question.

The relationship between the sacred and the secular is being drastically reinterpreted in contemporary theology. In the high Middle Ages the sacred was regarded as the fruition and completion of the secular. In the Lutheran Reformation the sacred and the secular were interpreted in terms of two kingdoms which were seen as being in conflict until the end of time; Luther said that the Christian must live out his vocation in the world but at the same time give his ultimate loyalty to the kingdom that is not of this world. Calvin also drew sharp and hard lines between the sacred and the secular, but he believed that the Christian armed with the Gospel message should seek to combat and convert the secular world. Modern secular or radical theology (Cox, van Buren, Robinson, William Hamilton) places the accent upon the identification and solidarity of the Christian with the world.[15] The lines between the holy and the profane are erased, since God or love is believed to be present in all men and in all places. Jesus is regarded no longer as the Savior from the principalities and powers of the world, but rather as a "contagious" model of human adulthood. In Tillich's theology the world is the church in its latency, and the distinctions between faith and unbelief are only relative. Barth maintains that the whole world is within the sphere of Christ's kingdom and that the kingdom of darkness has already been vanquished. In the thought of Karl Rahner the grace of Christ permeates everything, so that men always live consciously in the presence of this grace whether they believe in it or not.

Against the mainstream of contemporary theology I affirm that the world is a battleground between two opposing kingdoms—that of God and the demonic powers. The kingdom of God is hidden in the community of faith; consequently, the Christian is a warrior who seeks to extend God's realm in the world by witnessing to the Gospel in words and deeds. In opposition to the new secular theology I affirm that the sacred must never be identified with the secular, since the transcendence of God is thereby subverted. At the same time I contend that the secular, the sphere of man's relationships to finite realities, must always be related to and grounded in the sacred or the holy. The holy, moreover, should be equated not with a sacral or religious order of existence but with the Word of the transcendent and living God. The threat of secularism appears when the holy as a transcendent reality is either denied or identified with some religious symbol or activity.

With the Protestant Reformers I affirm an integral relationship between the holy and the profane. This relationship, however, must be viewed in terms of conflict rather than identification or even correlation. The church should seek to bring the world into obedience to the Lord Jesus Christ; against much of the older apologetics I hold that the Christian community should work for the radical conversion of secular culture rather than amalgamation with this culture. The Gospel message will always contravene the spirit of the age just as the church will always be a colony of heaven in a hostile world. The church can anticipate and witness to the coming kingdom; yet all orders and communities in this world will have to perish when God creates his world anew (Bonhoeffer). An apologetic which seeks to communicate to secular man by identifying the kingdom of God with the new metropolis (Winter) or the secular city (Cox) has betrayed the biblical testimony concerning the other-worldly character of the kingdom (John 18:36) and the radical ambiguity of all human ideals and achievements.

If theology is to maintain its integrity in a secular age it must again witness to the need for *diastasis* (separation) from cultural ideology and religion; at the same time it must call the world to a living faith in the God who transcends all human culture and history and who yet is active in this culture restraining men from perpetual warfare and redeeming men wherever his Word is obeyed.

II. Reappraising the Christian Witness

The problem of communicating the Gospel to the unbelieving world has become particularly acute since the advent of secularization. Yet this problem has been a perennial one, since the church has always been a minority movement within a culture that is more or less secular. What makes our situation different from that of other ages is that the church itself is becoming secular.[1] The need in our time is not only to reclaim the world for the Gospel but also to reconvert large segments of the church itself.

The problem of communication has various facets. First it involves the methodology of the theologian, that is, the method by which he seeks to determine the truth of the Christian faith. It also entails hermeneutics, which in its deepest sense can be said to be the translating of meaning (Bultmann). Finally it concerns apologetics and evangelism, or the defense and proclamation of the faith before the world.

In seeking to restate the Christian witness, theologians have been compelled to reinterpret both the truth-content of this witness and its cultural forms. Even Karl Barth, who seeks to remain true to the basic message of the faith affirmed by the church through the ages, nevertheless acknowledges that various teachings such as predestination and demonology have to be drastically revised.

Modern secular theology maintains that the categories of the Gospel must be translated into secular categories if it is to be made intelligible to modern man. Some theologians (such as Bonhoeffer) even suggest that the most potent testimony to Christ can be the wordless or silent ministry of suffering love.

The attempt to make the Christian witness plausible or acceptable to the outside world is known as apologetics.[2] The apologist for the faith seeks to convince the world of the credibility of the faith on the basis of a mutually acknowledged criterion (Tillich). What is important in the apologetic task and indeed indispensable is this "point of contact" between faith and unbelief.

It is debatable whether or not apologetics was a concern in the New Testament, but at least it was very prevalent in the early church period.[3] The church in the first several centuries found itself under fire from various pagan philosophies and religions. The apologists (Justin Martyr, Clement of Alexandria, and others) sought to answer the attacks of their critics, but they were unable to avoid a synthesis with classical pagan philosophy.

At the time of the Reformation apologetics came under severe criticism. Luther maintained that the Gospel is self-authenticating and therefore does not need outside supports.

> Thus conclude we that of God's Word can be no master or judge or any protector save God Himself. 'Tis His Word, and as He letteth it go forth without man's service and counsel, so will He hold and maintain it Himself for man's help and strength.[4]

Calvin allowed for the fact that a Christian could confirm his faith by the internal evidence of Scripture and the external evidences of nature, but in regard to the outside world only the evangelical proclamation could be of any value. He contended that the ministers of the Word should act as the prophets and apostles who "boast not their own genius, or any of those talents which conciliate the faith of the hearers; nor do they insist on arguments from reason." Rather they "bring forward the sacred name of God" which alone can penetrate the hearts of sinners.[5]

Apologetics appeared in a new form in post-Reformation orthodoxy. Orthodox theologians (like present-day fundamentalists) sought to utilize the ancient arguments for the existence of God and for the truth of revelation in order to convince the world of the plausibility of the claims of the revelation in Christ. At the same time they tried to avoid every kind of amalgamation with secular philosophy and endeavored always to demonstrate the superiority of Christian faith over secular thought.

Liberal Protestantism is based on the theological method known as modernism, which seeks to bring the Christian message into accord with modern thought and culture. Unlike the older classical apologetics, modernism seeks to effect a synthesis of Christian faith and secular philosophical meanings. Modernism may or may not be rationalistic in the narrow sense, but it is certainly based on the belief in man's capacity to find out the truth for himself. The foremost modernists of the 19th century were Schleiermacher and Ritschl, and in this century one might list Ernst Troeltsch, Emmanuel Hirsch, Shailer Mathews, and Henry Nelson Wieman. Modernism and fundamentalism, despite their seeming disparity, nevertheless are both based on an optimistic view of the sufficiency of human reason (understood in the broad sense of this term). Modernism is now under stricture even by those who still uphold the validity of the apologetic task.

One characteristic of contemporary Protestant theology is its consistent attack on rationalism and the older apologetics. This criticism is being made not only by biblical and confessional theologians but also by such radically philosophical thinkers as Wieman and Ogden. The theological critique of rationalism reflects the philosophical protest against it made by existentialists, Freudians, Marxists, and logical positivists, although the basis of this critique lies in another area. The revival of biblical studies in mainline liberal Protestantism has made theologians increasingly aware of the wide divergence between the dynamic Hebraic pattern of thinking and Hellenistic rationalism. The rediscovery of the witness of the Protestant Reformation concerning the depravity and corruption of man (including his reason) has also been a principal factor in this critique.

One other important influence should be mentioned in connection with the contemporary theological ferment. The writings of Søren Kierkegaard, the 19th century Danish religious philosopher, have only recently come to be appreciated by Christian thinkers and secular philosophers. His criticism was directed against both the speculative idealism of Hegel and the mediating theology which sought to combine Hegelian and biblical insights. Kierkegaard contended that Christianity consists not in rational conclusions but in existential life-and-death decisions. The Christian faith is based, he said, not on a metaphysical idea but on the act of God entering time, on the event of Jesus Christ which he called "the Absolute Paradox." This truth is not simply objective but rather objective-subjective; it is truth that can be grasped only by faith.

Kierkegaard was especially incensed at the mediating apologetic theology of his time, for he felt that it served to transform the event of salvation into a timeless idea. He averred: "These introductions succeed, because they introduce to a doctrine, but not to becoming a Christian." [6] And again:

> To make Christianity plausible is the same as to misinterpret it. And after all, what is it the free-thinkers want? Why they want to make Christianity plausible. . . . But the orthodox-apologetic effort also wants to make Christianity plausible, so it works hand in hand with heterodoxy.[7]

Yet Kierkegaard did not throw out all apologetics. He did criticize the direct method of communication, which simply presents a rational defense of faith. He suggested in its place a more indirect method which entails removing the illusions which keep men from treating Christianity seriously. Kierkegaard proceeded to puncture the idolatry in the theology and philosophy of his time; the principal illusion that must be shattered is the belief that we are already Christians. The point of contact with the Christian message, he held, is the temptation to despair, the consciousness of guilt. Only the Holy Spirit can convict men of their sin, but the apologist can unmask the hypocrisy by which men seek to cover their predicament. Among contemporary theologians who have been greatly influenced by Kierkegaard's indirect method of communication are Emil Brunner, Reinhold Niebuhr, and Paul Tillich.

Kierkegaard believed that the indirect method must finally give way to the direct method of evangelical proclamation. He regarded bearing witness to the truth as the goal of his labor: "The communication of Christianity must ultimately end in 'bearing witness,' the maieutic form can never be final. For truth, from the Christian point of view, does not lie in the subject . . . but in a revelation which must be proclaimed." [8] Kierkegaard insisted that this witness must be with life as well as with words; witnessing must finally take the form of bearing the cross as well as preaching.

A dominant segment of Protestant theology today is, like Kierkegaard, deeply critical of rationalism, particularly rationalistic apologetics. The arguments for the authority of the biblical revelation based on miracles and prophecy and the proofs for the existence of God have fallen into disrepute in all circles except scholastic orthodoxy. Brunner echoes the views of many theologians:

> There is no "proof" for revelation. Now the Church has very often made the mistake of offering "proofs" for revelation, which frequently provided easy targets for the attacks of rational criticism. A theology that allows itself to be drawn into producing proofs for its claim to revelation has already thrown up the sponge. It is the just punishment for the fact that it does not take its own subject and its own basis seriously.[9]

Tillich states that God cannot be proved because he is beyond existence. Barth contends that the only proof for faith is the proclamation of the faith. These men and others recognize that faith involves man's mind, but they also insist that a right mind must issue from a new heart. The task of communication must therefore take into account both the grace of God and the inherent depravity of man.

The older rationalistic apologetics is still maintained in some quarters. The Neo-Thomists continue to adhere to arguments for the existence of God, but at the same time they are reluctant to regard them as scientific proofs. Orthodox Protestant theology also retains the older apologetic approach; thinkers such as C. S. Lewis have given fresh and cogent expression to the classical proofs for God, revelation, and moral law. The apologetics of someone like John Gerstner appears to be much less convincing.[10] Yet even in the circles of orthodoxy much rethinking is being done concerning the role of apologetics today.

Many of the renewal theologians do not spurn apologetics completely, but like their mentor Søren Kierkegaard they seek a radical reappraisal of the apologetic task. They desire a new kind of apologetics, one that takes into account the sin and ambiguity in the life of man. They also wish to give full recognition to the historical character of revelation and to the uniqueness of Jesus Christ. Emil Brunner has called his theology a "missionary theology," one comprised of both proclamation and eristics (that kind of argumentation which does not defend the Gospel but instead takes the offensive against the opponent). Brunner's aim is to undercut the intellectual position of the nonbeliever and thereby drive him toward decision. The apologetics of Reinhold Niebuhr is similar in that he seeks to bring the pretensions of secular culture under the judgment of God. The Christian witness as reinterpreted by Niebuhr consists first of a critical analysis of the culture and then a pointing beyond the ambiguities of the culture to the grace of God revealed in the cross of Jesus Christ. Bultmann holds that we must demythologize the archaic picture language of the Bible and seek to communicate the message of the cross in the modern-day language of secular (existentialist) thought. Tillich addresses himself to the alienation and anxiety of modern man and then proceeds to point him to the Christian answer. All of these thinkers and also others including Richardson, Nygren, and Ferré can be placed in the category of the "new mediating theology" in that they seek to affirm the truth of faith and at the same time to demonstrate its relevance to secular man. It should be recognized that several of the so-called existentialist theologians have radically departed from the general approach of Kierkegaard and would indeed fall under his strictures against philosophical theology.

The secular or radical theologians can also be numbered among those who attempt to mediate between Christ and culture although their restatement of the apologetic task is somewhat different from that of Christian existentialists who dwell upon the guilt and estrangement of man. John Robinson, who in this respect has certain affinities with the later Bonhoeffer and Ebeling, states the case for a nonreligious interpretation of the Gospel. Others, such as Harvey Cox, hold that the key to communication today lies in the abandonment of the language of metaphysics for that of politics. Thomas Altizer's position is that only by acknowledging the death of God can the church today penetrate the thought world of secular man.

The radical theologians disavow the old style apologetics, but they nevertheless seek to make the faith contemporary and relevant and this means bringing it at least partially into accord with the spirit of the modern age.[11]

Another school of theology today has given up apologetics and endeavors instead to reach the nonbelieving world in another way. In this group are such men as Bonhoeffer, Barth, H. Richard Niebuhr, Kenneth Hamilton, and Arthur Cochrane. These men hold that a rational defense of the faith, however sophisticated and penetrating it might be, nevertheless fails to take seriously the nature of revelation as a personal encounter, and it also underestimates the blindness and helplessness of man apart from grace. Our task, according to these thinkers, is not to make the faith appealing to the modern consciousness but rather to bring the modern consciousness under the judgment of the truth of faith.

Bonhoeffer contends that apologetics is unchristian. It is both an attack upon the adulthood of the world and the practice of resting content with an allegedly secure place of retreat. Yet he maintains that the church is not to disengage itself from the problems and concerns of the world. "The Church must get out of her stagnation. We must move out again into the open air of intellectual discussion with the world, and risk shocking people if we are to cut any ice."[12] Bonhoeffer presents the case for an incarnational theology, one which seeks identification and solidarity with the suffering and the needy in the world. Our method of witnessing should be not simply preaching but a ministry of suffering love, a life lived under the cross. Here Bonhoeffer, despite his complete break with apologetics, has a basic affinity with Søren Kierkegaard.

Karl Barth's theology is concerned primarily with the explication and proclamation of the biblical message. Faith's appeal, he contends, should not be to a "point of contact" with unbelief but to the Holy Spirit. Theology must "renounce all apologetics or external guarantees of its position within the environment of other sciences, for it will always stand on the firmest ground when it simply *acts* according to the law of its own being."[13] Barth's theology is a kerygmatic theology, one based on the message of the cross and resurrection. This message can be made intelligible to modern man, he says, but only the Holy Spirit can make it knowable. According to Barth this message is the chosen means by which God reaches men. It stands on its own basis and needs no outside supports. We are called not to make the Word relevant but to discover the relevance already in the Word. Our responsibility is not to make the Word palatable to modern man, but to make it known to him. In Barth's view:

> What is involved is not the idle question of how those who proclaim this Word should "approach" this or that modern man, or how they should "bring home" the Word of God to him. Instead, the real question is how they have to *serve* this Word by pointing to its coming. This Word has never been "brought home" to any man except by its own freedom and power.[14]

Barth refuses to engage even in a negative apologetics. His motto is "Let God be God." This means that we should let God speak and act through his Word. Barth has been charged with cultural obscurantism by such men as Reinhold Niebuhr and Paul Tillich; yet even his severest critic will acknowledge that he has a lively interest in the thinking of the culture. He has been able to appreciate movements and values in the secular world because he perceives that the light of creation still shines even in the natural man, including his culture.

The question which we must finally consider is whether there can be an intelligible and compelling Christian witness apart from apologetics. Does not the attempt to move beyond apologetics pose the danger of ghettoism just as the older apologetics was tempted to syncretism? The Christian witness must be restated, but does not this entail a wrestling with unbelief as well as an explication of belief? The post-apologetic theologians would acknowledge the necessity for a full understanding of the secular thought of our time. Whether they are able to state their case more persuasively than the new mediating theologians remains to be seen.

III. *Karl Barth*

Karl Barth, professor emeritus at the University of Basel, Switzerland, has constructed a systematic theology which is oriented about the revelation and proclamation of the Word of God to a sinful world. Consequently, what he says is very relevant to the problem with which this book is concerned, namely, how to reach modern secular man with the Gospel.

Barth's theology is centered in the revelation of God in Jesus Christ as attested in the Bible. According to Barth, God apart from his revelation is inconceivable and inscrutable. He is nearer to us than we are to ourselves, yet he is hidden from us. God is known only as he gives himself to be known, and this means that he is known only in his freedom, only where he speaks his Word in the power of his Spirit.

In Barth's view man in himself is incapable of knowing God. He is prevented from knowing God not only because of his finitude as man but also and above all because of his sin. Man is ontologically related to God by virtue of the creation. He was created for obedience and not for rebellion, which is why Barth calls sin an "ontological impossibility." Yet sin nevertheless happened and continues to happen, so that the image of God in man has been marred, though not completely effaced. Sin does not change man's being but hides it. The plight of man is that he does not know his true self and therefore is constantly threatened by meaninglessness. The sinner is alienated from God, but he is not separated from God's love. He is plagued by fear and doubt, but he is still upheld by God. He is inwardly lost, but he is not rejected by God. Indeed God relates himself to all men at the very center of their being, and sin can obscure but not annul this fact.

Barth affirms that in Jesus Christ God has revealed himself to all men once and for all; this revelation is the ground and criterion of all truth. "The truth of Jesus Christ is not one truth among others; it is the truth, the universal truth that creates all truth as surely as it is the truth of God, the 'prima veritas' which is also the 'ultima veritas.'"[1] It is truth that cannot be grasped or attained by human reason. This truth stands in judgment over all human culture, religion, and philosophy.

The revelation of Christ signifies not only divine truth but also divine salvation. Indeed, in the cross and resurrection of Christ God has reconciled and justified the world. The cross reveals that darkness is excluded by God and has only provisional existence; the victory of Jesus Christ means that the kingdom of God is now established. The evil powers of darkness have been totally vanquished, and all men now find themselves within the sphere of the love and kingship of Jesus Christ. The final revelation of God's overwhelming victory over evil still remains to be disclosed, but the reality of this victory cannot be doubted.

According to Barth the Bible is the inspired witness to the revelation of Christ. It is also the unique channel by which this revelation becomes real for men of every age. Barth calls the Bible the written Word of God, but at the same time he will not identify it with revelation. When it is united by the Holy Spirit with the revealed Word of God which is Jesus Christ, then and then only does it become revelation for the believing community. Although Barth views the Bible as uniquely inspired, he nevertheless affirms its full humanity and its susceptibility to error. Still he regards the divine message of the Bible, the truth of salvation, as absolute and infallible.

Barth defines faith as the inner knowledge of divine revelation, a knowledge implanted in man by the Spirit of God. To be sure, in his theology faith consists not only in knowledge but also in trust and obedience. Yet he emphasizes the cognitive, rational character of faith. He writes that "what is certain is that faith must be described as knowledge and can also be described thus in its entirety." [2] Faith is the means by which man grasps the meaning of God's Word. The knowledge which faith has concerning its object is both indirect and incomplete; Barth insists that we never know Christ except in the sign, veil, and work of his redemptive acts in history. In other words, we meet only the hidden Christ, the Christ who is revealed in and at the same time veiled by the very fallible and broken witness of the Bible and the church.

Man has an openness to God's revelation because of his creation in God's image, yet because of his sin man does not have a readiness or willingness for this revelation. He has a yearning and longing but not a positive desire. He has an ontological freedom but not the practical freedom of coming to Christ. Therefore both the gift and the power to receive the gift are the work of God. Our justification consequently rests upon the free grace of God.

It is Barth's view that because Jesus Christ died for all men the possibility of believing in Christ is universal. All men are claimed for the kingdom. This possibility, however, is anchored in Christ and his Spirit, and not in the reason of man. The only "point of contact" is the Spirit himself who speaks and acts as he pleases. The Spirit may or may not choose human instruments and means to make known the truth of redemption. In Barth's mind human instruments are to be regarded not as necessary or sacramental means of grace but rather as tokens and signs of the free movement of the Spirit. Our preaching if it is faithful to the message of the Bible may be instrumental in confronting men with God's grace, but there is no guarantee of its effectiveness, for the Spirit is not bound to human means.[3]

Barth insists that faith is basically an acknowledgment of the salvation which was accomplished and actualized in Jesus Christ. It is not the act of faith but rather the atoning work of Christ that should be considered the salvation-event. "It [faith] is not the event of the redemptive act of God. It can only follow this. It is subsequent and at the deepest possible level subordinate to it." [4] Faith is an inward awakening to this salvation, and thereby it also brings us into contact with the victory of Christ. Barth maintains that all men are saved and elected through the death and resurrection of Christ; the mission of the church is to confront the world with this fact and to call the world to begin to live out of gratefulness for this salvation. He writes against modern preaching: "The emphasis in much of today's preaching has to do with salvation in the future, something the preacher can help give, instead of speaking of the perfect salvation already accomplished. We only await its final revelation." [5]

Barth holds that we can make the Gospel intelligible by demonstrating its internal coherence, but that we cannot make it knowable. Since the Gospel is not an axiom of reason it cannot be demonstrated by logic. Since it is not a datum of experience it cannot be validated by appealing to the findings of empirical science. There can be no convincing arguments for the existence of God nor for the validity of his revelation. Barth will therefore have nothing to do with apologetics in the traditional sense. The truth of faith is self-authenticating; it needs logical explication but not rational supports. The Gospel "cannot be recommended and defended; it has no advocates and no propagandists." [6] It can only be attested to and presented. We should preach the Gospel clearly and intelligibly and in the language of the people, but we must not seek to build bridges between the truth of faith and secular philosophy. We should relate our message to the political and social upheavals of our time, yet we should preach not a social Gospel but the Gospel of the cross.[7]

Barth has insisted that the oral witness must be united with the ministry of love and service. Speech and action must be distinguished, but they can never be separated. This means that we are called not only to address the world but also to identify ourselves with the world in its misery and anguish. He affirms: "Without this active solidarity with the least of little ones, without this concrete witness to Jesus the Crucified . . . its [the church's] witness may be ever so pure and full at other points, but it is all futile." [8]

It is Barth's conviction that we should view our hearers not as children of the devil but as children of God. We should regard them not as miserable sinners but as virtual brothers.[9] We should declare our solidarity with them in both sin and grace. The herald of the Gospel should ignore the fact that his hearers may be unbelievers. He is not to seek common ground with them, for all men already stand on common ground. This is not because men have an innate capacity to respond to the Gospel, but rather because all men have the image of God. This image, however, is not a property they possess but rather a relationship to God which rests upon God's unmerited grace.

Barth's theology is kerygmatic rather than apologetic. This means that he seeks to reach the world primarily through proclamation rather than argumentation. He recognizes that the existence of God can be demonstrated to faithful reason but not to the world. His methodology is similar to that of Anselm—faith seeking understanding. Anselm is regarded by Barth as one of his spiritual forebears. Barth holds that we must seek to understand our faith in the light of the criticisms of secular philosophy, but this does not mean that we should mix what cannot be mixed, namely, faith and unbelief. Because even the Christian continues in sin, his proclamation will forever be weakened and darkened by some philosophy or ideology; nevertheless it is through a fallible human proclamation that God makes known his infallible Word.

Barth's theology is a theology of revelation rather than a natural theology. He does not build on what is given in experience or generally acknowledged by the world; instead he seeks to explicate and herald what is declared in Holy Scripture. In the light of revelation we can see the work of God in creation. Indeed, the redemption by Christ confirms and fulfills God's redemptive purpose in creation.

* * * * *

In making a theological appraisal of Barth's position I am limiting myself to those particular doctrines which have a direct bearing on the communication of the Gospel to the world today. First of all, let us examine the doctrine of salvation as it is enunciated by Barth. Barth's view that *everything* pertaining to our salvation has already been accomplished by Jesus Christ can be questioned. To be sure, the decisive battle has been fought and won against the powers of darkness, but the warfare certainly continues. Yet Barth often speaks as if the war itself were over, as if the kingdom of darkness has been eradicated. His stress is on the saving work of Christ in the past, but does not salvation also have a present and future dimension?

Barth emphasizes the objective reality and total efficacy of the reconciling work of God in Christ. For him the present pole of salvation is simply an acknowledgment of what has already happened in the past. The future pole is nothing other than the revelation of what has already been accomplished by Christ. Faith, therefore, is basically subsequential and nonfundamental; it follows a salvation that has already been realized for all men in all times. This means that in our preaching we are to tell people that they have already been saved and are even now children of God. Barth holds that since the death and resurrection of Christ there are no real outsiders. He is sharply critical of those who speak of a totally secularized "man come of age":

> . . . we cannot at all reckon in a serious way with *real* "outsiders," with a "world come of age," but only with a world which *regards* itself as of age . . . the so-called "outsiders" are really only "insiders" (who have not yet understood and apprehended themselves as such).[10]

Barth's view seems to contradict the assertion frequently made in the New Testament that there is a division between faith and unbelief, between the children of light and the children of darkness (cf. Luke 16:8; John 8:44-47; Rom. 9-8; Eph. 5:6-8; 1 John 3:10). It is true that many passages point to the universal triumph of the grace of God, yet this truth can be affirmed while at the same time recognizing the role of faith in salvation. Barth believes that "all men and all creation . . . are ordained to be the theaters of His glory and therefore to be the recipients and bearers of His Word." [11] He recognizes, however, that only believers can be counted as members of the covenant community. I agree that all men are claimed for the kingdom by virtue of the sacrifice of Christ; yet it must be stressed that only those who have faith in Christ actually enter into the glory and freedom of the kingdom. All men are beneficiaries of the death of Jesus Christ, but they benefit in different ways. Those who spurn the offer of the Gospel are made servants of the King even against their wills, whereas those who believe in Christ become his sons and daughters.

This brings us to the question of whether Barth fully understands the gravity of man's predicament. In Barth's theology man is integrally related to God by virtue of the creation; this relationship is confirmed, strengthened, and fulfilled by the saving work of Christ. But this means that man is never really lost.[12] It also means that the new birth is basically a change in perspective rather than a change in being. Barth does not deny that in faith men begin to reflect their new being in Christ, but the contrast between the believer and the unbeliever is a relative one, for even the unbeliever is in continuity with God in Christ. Sin, then, is for Barth a state of blindness rather than a state of ontological corruption and incapacity. For Barth the devil is not a rebellious angelic being with positive power but rather a negative reality which has been overthrown by Jesus Christ. The devil's actual power is illusory; that is to say, it lies basically in our minds. Here one can discern Barth's affinity with the Enlightenment. Our liberation is said to consist in rational illumination or knowledge, although admittedly this knowledge is given by the Spirit of God. Barth also approaches the Enlightenment in his affirmation of the universal light within all men, his emphasis on the rationality of faith, his belief in the inevitable triumph of the good, and his understanding of the sacraments as signs and pledges rather than supernatural means of grace.

I can appreciate Barth's stress on the uniqueness and self-authenticating character of revelation. His insistence that the knowledge of faith is given only in and through revelation marks his theology as biblical rather than philosophical. His view that apologetics cannot be an introduction to the work of dogmatics is refreshing in a time when too much theology is still being built upon a rationalistic philosophy of religion. Barth, even though he opposes apologetics in the traditional sense, nevertheless sees the need to wrestle with the questions of culture. But at the same time he contends that our purpose should be not to discover a point of contact with the answer of faith but rather to show to what degree these questions fall short of the question of faith.

Perhaps Barth overemphasizes the rational character of revelation and faith. His concern in his later writings is to maintain the continuity between revelation and reason; he even holds that the truth of revelation confirms rather than overthrows reason understood as common sense. But he should recognize that faith also has a mystical or non-rational dimension. Faith is not only knowledge but also an experience which involves self-transcendence and the abdication of reason. Barth tends to underplay the volitional aspect of faith; his emphasis particularly in his later works is on faith as knowledge and trust rather than as a decision which entails venture and risk.

As far as Barth's theology of preaching is concerned, I must question whether the ambassador of Christ is to preach only the good news, the message of grace; should he not proclaim bad news as well, that is, the law and judgment of God? Barth holds that in addressing the world we must proclaim only God's love and his work of reconciliation. The law can be preached to Christians but not primarily as a means of driving them to repentance; instead the law is a guideline for the Christian life. According to Barth the law comes not before but after the Gospel. But do not the Gospel and law belong together, and must we not always preach the whole counsel of God, judgment as well as salvation?

Barth maintains that our concern as preachers should not be to save souls but to exalt Christ and glorify God. He reminds us that salvation is not ours to give. We are heralds and not saviors, servants of grace but not means of grace. We are simply to point our hearers to the grace of God which has already effected their salvation. He writes concerning the role of preaching:

> Even with the most powerful and heartfelt appeal which it may make to them, it cannot change men. But with its appeal it can set before them the act of the love of God in which He has already changed them.[13]

Is Barth sound in his judgment that the preacher of the Gospel is only a herald and witness and not also a channel and agent of the salvation of God? Paul said: "I have become all things to all men, that I might by all means save some" (1 Cor. 9:22). Another apostle wrote: "And convince some who doubt; save some, by snatching them out of the fire" (Jude 22, 23, cf. 1 Tim. 4:16; James 5:20). Barth acknowledges that men may be given transforming peace and inward confidence through preaching, and this too must be understood as one of the goals or aims of the Christian mission. Yet he contends that this does not mean that we actually bring men *salvation* in our preaching. Nor does it mean that the main purpose of evangelism is the edification of man. For Barth the goal of evangelistic preaching must always remain the uplifting of the crucified and risen Savior, Jesus Christ.

IV.
Emil Brunner

Emil Brunner's theology, much more than Barth's, is oriented about the problem of the secularization of the modern world. He affirms: "More and more I come to the view that the church nowadays speaks not chiefly to Christians, as it did in the Middle Ages and at the time of the Reformation and even a hundred years ago; it must speak primarily to 'heathen.'"[1] Brunner sees his theology as a "missionary theology," one that endeavors to make the Gospel a live option for secular men. Brunner was a pastor, a theological professor (at the University of Zurich), and a missionary-teacher in Japan.

One problem which has continually occupied him is the relationship of revelation and reason. He defines reason as any cognitive faculty within man. Reason, he maintains, is incapable of arriving at ultimate truth because of man's creatureliness and also because of his sinfulness. Brunner describes sin as a revolt against God, a revolt which discolors man's sensitivities and powers of cognition particularly in the area of his relationship with God. Sin is total, but unequal; that is to say, it does not affect every area of man's life to the same degree. Thinking in the empirical world of objects is only slightly tainted by sin, but in the area of ultimate concern man's reason is greatly clouded. Brunner makes a distinction between "world-knowledge" and "God-knowledge." In the former, reason preserves a degree of autonomy, but in the area of God-knowledge reason is hopelessly confused. He makes it clear that it is not reason in itself that opposes the Word of God but rather the arrogance of reason. It is the direction of reasoning, not the structure of reason, that is infected by sin.

It is Brunner's view that natural reason, reason apart from the grace of revelation, is incapable of coming to an adequate knowledge of God. Yet he says that natural reason is capable of arriving at a broken knowledge of God. Brunner therefore upholds the possibility of a natural knowledge of God and even of a natural theology. This natural knowledge, though, cannot be used as preparation for a theology of revelation. Nevertheless, our natural knowledge of God points to the true God and reminds us of our original union with him. This natural knowledge is correlative with original or general revelation. It is not saving but condemning knowledge; it gives us enough light to make us inexcusable in the sight of God.

Brunner maintains that this natural knowledge makes us capable of hearing the Word of God. In his debate with Barth on natural theology he spoke of an addressability in man, a capacity for words, which Barth interpreted as a capacity for revelation.[2] Whatever Brunner meant by this, we must recognize that he affirms a point of contact between revelation and reason, between God and man. This point of contact is none other than man's conscience or sense of guilt.

Revelation is interpreted in terms of a divine-human encounter, an encounter which became decisive in the incarnation of God in Jesus. The divine-human encounter occurs anew whenever men meet the risen Christ through the power of the Holy Spirit. Brunner holds that the subject-object antithesis characterizes the natural mode of knowledge. Natural reason cleaves either to idealism, which locates reality in the subject, or to materialism, which locates reality in the object, that is, in nature. Pantheism is the result of reason seeking to posit an underlying unity between subject and object. In Christian revelation, Brunner contends, the subject-object antithesis is transcended; there is an identity of subject and object in faith. In revelation man no longer encounters an object but a living subject, Jesus Christ. Faith, then, is the union of spiritual immediacy and historical mediacy.

The locus of authority in Brunner's theology is the conjunction of Word and Spirit. Pietism and mysticism, he says, tend to derive their truth only from subjective experience, that is, from the Spirit.

Orthodoxy, on the other hand, locates truth in the Word, which when separated from the Spirit becomes a dead letter. Brunner maintains that we must move beyond both objectivism and subjectivism to dialectical theology, which alone can hold together the objective event and the subjective illumination.

Faith is the response of the Christian to revelation. It is based upon the Word of God and not upon experience. Brunner makes this affirmation against mysticism. At the same time he holds that faith is realized in experience. Indeed, faith is itself an experience—the experience of the Spirit of Christ. But this experience is not an absorption into God but an encounter with God. In opposition to the mystics, he contends that fellowship with God, not union with a ground of being, is the goal of Christian faith. Brunner's theology, then, is basically existential and personalistic.

Brunner agrees with Barth that the Bible is not itself revelation but rather a witness to revelation. It contains the authentic interpretation of God's will and purpose for the world, but this does not mean that everything in the Bible can be accepted as the literal truth. (Brunner himself disputes the doctrines of the Virgin Birth of Christ and the Ascension.) The Bible is not only the norm of faith but also its source; we believe in God because he speaks to us through the Bible.

Brunner maintains that faith stands only on its own criterion, on the Word of God. It provides its own evidence—the assurance of forgiveness. Faith is always accompanied by doubt, but faith itself is characterized by certainty. Doubt, he says, is the intellectual form of sin. Yet faith is an inner certainty, not an objective or rational certainty. It is not an assured possession but a process of continually becoming sure.

The content of revelation is Jesus Christ and his salvation, including both the forgiveness of sins and the new creation. At the same time regeneration is only begun in this life; the Christian always remains a sinner. The Christian life is not a matured possession of victory but rather an unceasing struggle toward victory. In Brunner's view the reconciling work of God in Christ brings to us only the possibility of salvation. The saving work of the cross must be appropriated in the decision of faith if salvation is to become ours. Salvation, like revelation, is interpreted in objective-subjective rather than in purely objective terms. Brunner's orientation is dialectical and existential rather than simply historical.

Salvation, moreover, has a definite eschatological orientation. Brunner reminds us that faith itself is not the solution, but that it knows of a future solution. Faith is not the possession of salvation but the possession of the promise of salvation. Brunner's eschatology is basically futuristic, although he does acknowledge the new life as a present reality.

The church is the community founded on the event of salvation. Yet the church signifies for Brunner the institutionalization of spiritual religion, the objectifying of faith. The hope of the church today lies not in the institution but in the *ecclesia,* the collection of living cells of Christian fellowship within and outside the church. The ideal church is not the institution but the gathered community. The sacraments are ordinances, not means of salvation; only the Word is the means of salvation. Wherever the Word is rightly preached and rightly heard, there we have the true church.

How is the Word to be communicated to the world? What is needed, Brunner contends, is a missionary theology which has two aspects—eristics and evangelical proclamation. Eristics is Brunner's term for the method of attack. This method is to be distinguished from traditional apologetics, which sought to defend the faith against attack through rational proofs. The new apologetics must take the offensive against an arrogant and presumptuous culture. Its task is to overthrow the position of unbelief and drive our hearers into despair.

Brunner also adheres to the so-called "method of correlation," by which he seeks to conjoin the questions of culture and the answer of faith. He writes concerning the need for correlation:

> The one fundamental task of the theologian is to so understand the Gospel that it answers the questions of men of every "present age." If he does not do this, if he ignores the questions of the man of today, then he is ignoring the living man himself and failing to capture his attention.[3]

Yet in his view the method of correlation must serve eristics. This means that the purpose of the apologist should be not only to demonstrate the validity of the Christian answer but also to point out the fallacies and deficiencies in the self-understanding of the culture.

In his apologetics Brunner finds his point of contact with natural man in man's sense of lostness, which may or may not lead to a consciousness of sin or to repentance. The despairing knowledge of distress and need, the awareness of sin, comes from the law of God. Despair is the soil out of which faith grows. When we despair of ourselves, then we are ready to make the leap of faith. At the same time he recognizes that there is no inevitable progression from despair to faith.

The Gospel cannot be proved, but we can at least show how the Gospel is a live alternative for modern man. We can demonstrate the inadequacies of the philosophical answers and the validity of the Christian answer. The apologetic task is feasible because the Gospel signifies the fulfillment of man's deepest yearnings and man's existential quest.

* * * *

In the appraisal of Brunner's theology it should first be pointed out that he is equivocal in regard to natural theology. He sometimes denies its validity, but in other places he holds that it is important. "Though it may not be the basis, it still is a very important part of Christian Theology, especially in the doctrine of man."[4] Brunner is not a natural theologian in the classical sense, for he does not affirm a universal natural law. Nevertheless he still speaks of orders of creation; he acknowledges the possibility of a natural knowledge of God and holds that such knowledge can be a link with the revelation of Jesus Christ. He speaks of a general revelation in which God is only dimly revealed; I wonder, though, if we can speak of revelation unless God is truly or fully revealed.

Brunner's distinction between theology and philosophy is patently artificial. Theology, he contends, is the discipline that treats of the nature and purpose of God as revealed in Jesus Christ. A Christian philosophy refers to the speculation of Christian thinkers on the problem of being and the origins of the cosmos. Is not Heidegger more sound when he claims that a Christian philosophy is a "round square" and a "misunderstanding"?[5] Philosophy ceases to be philosophy when autonomous reason is not taken as the final authority, and theology is woefully deficient unless it relates biblical insights to the basic problems and questions of man. It is interesting to note that Nygren accuses Brunner of capitulating to the I-Thou philosophy of Martin Buber.[6]

This brings us to Brunner's doctrine of revelation. Is revelation principally a personal address, as he contends, or does it not also contain a rational element? Brunner acknowledges that the message of faith is not only address and claim but also the communication of meaning. Yet by divorcing faith and reflection he is unable to affirm that objective, rational truth is communicated in revelation. Brunner is of course correct in his view that the knowledge of faith is not itself doctrine, but he does not discern the continuity between faith and doctrine. He openly questions the doctrines of the Trinity, the Virgin Birth, and the Ascension of Christ, even though these are attested in Scripture (either explicitly or implicitly). Brunner could be accused of reductionism, of reducing the content of revelation to the assurance of the forgiveness of sins and the new life in Christ.

Just as he separates faith and doctrine so Brunner also tends to separate faith and experience. Faith, he maintains, is based on the Word of God and not on experience. He acknowledges that faith is realized in experience, that faith might even be regarded as an experience, but he takes pains to point out that this experience is to be understood in terms of personal encounter rather than of mysticism. Yet is the I-Thou encounter simply a meeting of minds and not also a blending of personalities? Bonhoeffer has written that in the I-Thou encounter the Thou enters into the subject as an I.[7] Brunner is outspoken in his denunciation of mysticism, and yet he holds to the identity of subject and object in the experience of faith, an earmark of mystical religion.

In his Christology Brunner affirms as the basis of faith "the historic Jesus, the Christ and Saviour of the Biblical message" as opposed to the historical Jesus of liberalism and the Christ of orthodoxy.[8] Yet there are traces of Nestorianism and even docetism in Brunner's theology. He tends to separate the humanity and deity of Christ; he sometimes refers to Jesus as the mask of Christ. He refuses to affirm the Virgin Birth and thereby opens the door to adoptionism, although this is not his avowed intention. He acknowledges the resurrection of the living Christ but not the bodily resurrection of Jesus; he also denies the preexistence of Jesus and his literal ascension.

Brunner also appears to sever the living Christ from the church. He will not acknowledge the church as the mystical body of Christ. The true church in his theology is the ecclesia or fellowship of love which he does not relate in any meaningful way to the visible church.

The strength of Brunner's theology is that it holds together the objective and subjective poles of salvation. He perceives the biblical truth that salvation is to be located not only in God's reconciling work in Christ but also in our decision in and for Christ. Salvation, though, means for him the forgiveness of sins and restoration to fellowship with God rather than inward mystical transformation and sanctification. The message of faith as he sees it is the justification of the ungodly, not the transformation of men. Brunner's theology, like Barth's and Niebuhr's, is more a *theologia crucis* than a *theologia gloriae*. There is truth in this position, but must we not also affirm the *theologia gloriae*, since we hold to both the cross and the resurrection?

This brings us to Brunner's apologetics. He calls his theology a missionary rather than a church theology. He acknowledges that our commission is to address both the church and the world, but should our address take the form of an apologia or of an evangelical proclamation? Brunner desires an apologia as a preparation for proclamation, but I question whether we can penetrate the barrier of unbelief through our own skills and wisdom in defending the Gospel. Brunner's missionary theology is an anthropology, for its point of departure is not Christ but rather man. He has declared: "From this standpoint, then, we can understand the fact . . . that anthropology, the self-understanding of man, is and must be the real place for discussion between the Christian Faith and non-Christian thought." [9]

Brunner recognizes that only the Holy Spirit can bring faith, but he insists that the preacher can awaken a thirst for the Spirit within his hearers by showing them how Christ meets their deepest needs.

He holds that we can remove false barriers to belief and thereby open the way for the coming of the Spirit.

He contends that our message can find a hearing because of man's inherent sense of guilt. Every man, he says, has a faint but sure awareness that he stands under the condemnation of the law. Consequently he is impelled to seek the Gospel of righteousness even though he cannot through his own power commit himself to it.[10] But does man really seek for God on his own, particularly if faith is not present? Does a consciousness of guilt lead necessarily to a consciousness of sin? Brunner maintains that the knowledge of guilt is possible for the natural man, but that a knowledge of sin can be had only in the presence of God. He affirms: "Only in the Mediator Jesus Christ do we know ourselves as we really are." [11]

Brunner calls his approach "eristics," which describes the method of attack. Eristics consists in overthrowing the bastions of unbelief. It involves undercutting false faith and undermining false religion. He points to 2 Cor. 10:5, where Paul says that we are commanded to overthrow arguments. But in Paul's mind the means for overthrowing arguments is the proclamation of the Gospel, not an eristical apologetics. According to Paul we are to preach good news, not drive the natural man into deeper despair. In Brunner's view the man in despair is ripe for the true faith. But cannot despair lead as often to suicide as it does to salvation? Should not a distinction be made between the sorrow of this world which produces death and the sorrow for our sins which comes only by knowing of the love of Christ? (cf. 2 Cor. 7:1). Brunner says that humanity "is more ready to listen to this answer" today than in other periods of history because of the present social upheavals and the demise of the older faiths.[12]

Brunner acknowledges that authentic witnessing consists in telling the story of salvation. He is very adamant at this point: "The revelation of God must be *told,* not *taught;* the doctrine only has validity as a means of serving the 'telling' of the Good News." [13] Brunner's sermons are basically evangelical and kerygmatic. Yet his apologetic concern has misled him into seeking to conjoin *witnessing* in the biblical sense and argumentation. He has been led to appeal to both the power of the Gospel and man's uneasy conscience or sense of lostness. The question is whether man's natural sense of lostness can enable him to understand or even to seek the Gospel of redemption. I hold that what is needed is the light and power of the Holy Ghost, which alone can break down the defenses of natural man and make him ready and willing to receive the salvation of Jesus Christ.

Brunner can be appreciated in this time when the Gospel is being confused with a political platform and social program. He has remained faithful to the biblical teaching that the mission of the church is the proclamation of the Gospel of eternal salvation rather than the building of a this-worldly utopia. He has held that a pronounced emphasis on social amelioration is a symptom of the church's weakness, since the Gospel is essentially spiritual and personal although having social and secular implications. According to Brunner the primary task of the church is not to change or improve the social order but rather "to preach the Gospel of Jesus Christ, the Kingdom of God which transcends all social orders. . . ."[14] Brunner does not mean to imply that Christians should not become involved in the social and political crises of the time; yet such involvement should be seen as a fruit and consequence of the church's spiritual mission, not an integral element in it. This perspective sorely needs to be recovered in our time.

V.
Rudolf Bultmann

Rudolf Bultmann was professor for many years in the field of New Testament studies at the University of Marburg, Germany. He was originally associated with the movement known as "the theology of crisis," which also included Barth and Brunner. But Bultmann has since moved away in the direction of an existential theology rather than a theology of the Word of God. His concern has been the predicament of man and the breakthrough into authentic existence, not the universal cosmic triumph of grace. Bultmann's theology has been a decisive influence upon the new hermeneutic movement associated with the names of Ernst Fuchs, Gerhard Ebeling, and Hans-Georg Gadamer.

Bultmann's theology is centered in the kerygma, the message of the cross. He states that the criterion of faith must be taken not from the modern world-view but from an existential understanding of the New Testament. He insists, however, that the existential truth of the New Testament must be distinguished from its mythical form. In his mind one of the principal reasons why the kerygma is rejected by modern secular men is that it is confused with an outdated mythology. He asserts: "The Church can re-establish communication with modern man and speak with an authentic voice only after she has resolutely abandoned mythology." [1] We should no longer, he maintains, preach the cross as a sacrifice for sins, the bodily resurrection of Christ from the grave and the nature-miracles of Christ, for these are all products of mythological thinking. Rather we should preach the agonizing death on the cross and the new life that accrues to those who find in the cross the forgiveness of sins. We should preach *sola gratia* and *sola fide*, the message that we are justified solely by the free grace of God, which is received only by faith.

Bultmann holds that we must proclaim the cross as an eschatological event, an event which confronts us in the present and opens up a new future for us. The *eschaton* is not the end of the physical world but the end of one's own life in the decision of faith. He acknowledges that in the cross of Jesus Christ God was acting for our redemption. An objective power was released in the world, the power of vicarious suffering love. The cross of Christ is the revelation that God is merciful; the cross brings to us the possibility of freedom from bondage to the law and sin. The stories of the resurrection are simply attempts to explain the meaning of the cross. The resurrection experiences are nothing other than experiences of the cross.

The heart of the Christian message according to Bultmann is not the historical Jesus but the "Christ event," which consists not only in the historical death of Christ but also in the proclamation of this death and the acceptance of this message.[2] We meet the living Christ not in the Jesus of history but in the preached word of the cross. The decision to which we are called is accepting the fact that we have been accepted. We are called to forsake our own righteousness and cast ourselves on the righteousness of Christ; in this decision we become free from care, sin and lust. We also are given a true understanding of ourselves. Bultmann's emphasis is on faith as decision. But he holds that faith consists also in obedience, in a life lived under the cross. Faith is not objective knowledge but trust in and life-long loyalty to the crucified and living Savior.

Bultmann concerns himself with the problem of how to make the Christian message intelligible to the post-Christian man. He writes that his purpose "is not to make religion more acceptable to modern man by trimming the traditional Biblical texts, but to make clearer to modern man what the Christian faith is."[3] He recognizes that people today are living in a scientific secularized world.

The main problem in Christian theology is consequently one of translation, the hermeneutical problem. Bultmann sees existential philosophy as a very important aid in the task of theological translation. Existential philosophy, particularly Heidegger's philosophy, can help us to describe the fallenness and despair of man. It can enable us to present the kerygma as a theoretical possibility for modern man. Only grace, though, can enable men to appropriate the kerygma so that it becomes a practical reality in their lives. He is very insistent on this point:

> For the possibility of living by the grace of God can, by its very nature, be given only to me; it is not a possibility open to all for the taking. If it were, the very meaning of the revelation —the grace given to man who is nothing before God—would be lost.[4]

Bultmann acknowledges a point of contact between the Gospel and the natural man, namely, the recognition of man's guilt and anxiety. Philosophy can help us toward this recognition, although the Christian faith will necessarily interpret man's predicament in a slightly different way than secular philosophy will. The point of contact is therefore also a point of conflict. Bultmann accepts natural theology as an interpretation of pre-faith existence from the standpoint of faith. But like Barth he refuses to accept natural theology as a basis for a theology of revelation. Nevertheless, pre-faith existence can know much about the real condition of man. Christian revelation confirms the non-Christian inquiry about God and man but refutes the non-Christian answer.

Bultmann's main contribution to the contemporary discussion lies in his plea for demythologizing the biblical myths so that the authentic message of the faith can be proclaimed. He defines myth as an anthropological way of speaking about divinity in order to attain an understanding of self and environment.[5] Since a myth is anthropological it is necessarily conditioned by the culture which produced it; moreover, it refers to abstract divinity rather than to the living reality of God which can be experienced in the here and now. Myth "objectifies the divine activity and projects it on the plane of worldly happenings," whereas true miracles are hidden from sight and revealed only to faith.[6] Myth is basically pre-scientific imagery, he maintains, and is therefore no longer valid in a scientific secular age. It is permissible, even mandatory, to demythologize, because this process was started in the New Testament itself. To demythologize is to reinterpret the myth, but not to replace it with another myth.

What is the content of a Gospel that has been demythologized? According to Bultmann, such a Gospel is none other than the message of God's love revealed in Jesus Christ. It is certainly not mythical speculation concerning a pre-existent Christ, blood sacrifice, the virgin birth, a ransom to Satan, etc. Our gospel must concern the living Christ rather than the mythological Christ. The crucifixion and resurrection have meaning for us mainly as present experiences. We must preach not that Jesus literally rose from the dead but that he rose into the hearts of believers. He continues to live not in some transcendent heaven but in the kerygma, the evangelical proclamation. The experience of the resurrection is none other than the encounter with the Christ of the kerygma. The end of the world in a demythologized gospel is not the second coming of Christ at the end of history but the end of non-authentic existence and the opening of a new future, an event which takes place in the crisis of repentance and faith. The content of revelation is the experience of forgiveness, not supranatural knowledge. Revelation is an occurrence rather than illumination or doctrine. Salvation consists in the realization of authentic existence rather than a vicarious substitutionary sacrifice for sin. Salvation is a practical (ontic) possibility for men, he maintains, in the encounter with the kerygma. Here Bultmann diverges from some of his more radical disciples such as Ogden and Buri, who maintain that the realization of authentic life is a universal ever-present possibility.[7]

* * * * *

Bultmann's understanding of mythology is not exempt from criticism. He reminds us that myth is not in itself the Christian message. It is even possible to accept the myth and reject the claims of faith (as does Karl Jaspers). The question that we must consider, though, is whether one can accept the message and yet reject the myth.

Bultmann maintains that the ancient world view has been discredited by modern science. That is not really the central issue, however; we must distinguish between religious truths and world pictures, between the *Weltanschauung* and the *Weltbild.* Aulén, for example, holds that we must penetrate behind imagery to dynamic religious ideas and themes. The concepts of sin-sacrifice, the last judgment, the virgin birth, and the devil are religious truths; this is the realm of faith. We should recognize that it is not the biblical world picture that is scandalous to the self-understanding of the natural man but rather the Christian faith itself.

Bultmann affirms that the myth has been discredited by history. But the fact that the final event of history did not happen at the time it was expected does not mean that it will never happen. Jesus himself affirmed that no man shall know the day or the hour. Realized or "realizing" eschatology, when conceived in a radical exclusive sense, betrays the Christian faith. Even the Fourth Gospel, which emphasizes eternal life in the present, holds to a futuristic eschatology as well (cf. John 5:25-29; 6:39, 40, 44, 54).

Bultmann contends that there are internal discrepancies in the biblical myths. But the differences in theological formulation in the New Testament must be viewed as differences in emphasis due to the various modes of accommodation of the Holy Spirit. There is no real contradiction, for example, between John's view of the Christian hope and that of the Synoptic Gospels. Nor is there a fundamental discrepancy between the kenosis passage in Philippians and the accounts in the Synoptic Gospels of Jesus the miracle worker. Within and behind the historical relativity and doctrinal divergence can be seen a unity of divine revealing action and faith-response. We must acknowledge, however, that the absolute perspective belongs to God alone; the systematic theologian can hope only for a coherent but relative perspective.

Part of Bultmann's trouble is that he does not adequately differentiate between knowing and being. For him the risen Christ is the power of the new life proclaimed in the church. But did not an objective historical resurrection occur prior to our existential decision? Myth describes the objectivity of the workings of God, and is not this objectivity the ground and basis of the subjective response of faith? Knowing communicates being, to be sure, but is not being prior to knowing?

Bultmann's view that the imagery of the myth is culturally con-

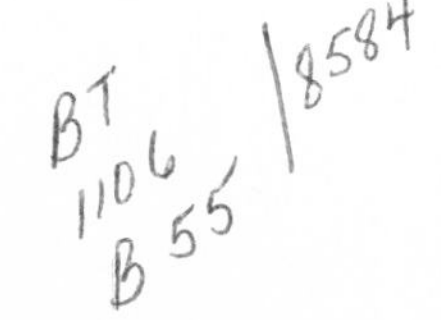

ditioned must be taken seriously; this is a fact that cannot be gainsaid. Yet we must insist that although the picture language of the Bible is derived from the culture of that time, the meaning-content which this language points to transcends the culture and history of that or any period.

This brings us to Bultmann's position that myth is anthropological in nature, that its concern is to enable man to understand himself more fully. Actually the New Testament myth is not anthropological but unabashedly theological; its concern is with God's decisive redemptive action in a particular history. The mythical form of language is consequently indispensable, for the action of divinity cannot be adequately described in strictly logical and scientific terminology.

Much of the confusion concerning the nature of myth would be overcome if we distinguished between two different kinds of myths. First there is the revelational myth, which is an imaginative symbolic description of what God declares to be true. Because this kind of myth is oriented about God's creative and redemptive action in history, it might also be called sacred saga.[8] There is also the ideological myth, a symbolic description of what man imagines to be true. This type of myth is centered in a universal truth, one which may, however, have historical implications.

Unlike the myths of antiquity, the New Testament myth is concerned with historical revelation. If myth be defined as speaking about divinity in terms of this world, is there any other way in which we can speak about the action of God? [9] Prenter contends that when the mythical vision is abandoned, metaphysics or psychology takes its place.[10] In Bultmann's case it would seem that psychology has supplanted mythology; his psychology is disguised in existential terminology. The crucifixion and resurrection become facts in the "soul" or in "existence."

Bultmann is right in saying that we must seek to demythologize in the sense of trying to penetrate behind the biblical imagery to its meaning. Nevertheless, our interpretation must be based not on secular criteria but on the Gospel message itself. If it is true that meaning conditions language from within and that the only language that can adequately describe the action of God is mythical or imaginative symbolic language, then we cannot wholly abandon what Barth calls "the language of Canaan" even though we must seek to interpret it in modern-day terms.

This brings us to an appraisal of Bultmann's existential theology. He himself admits that his concern is to replace theology with anthropology. "I am trying to substitute anthropology for theology, for I am interpreting theological affirmations as assertions about human life."[11] But this amounts to a kind of reductionism after the pattern of Ritschl. It was Ritschl who reduced the great themes of the faith to value-judgments.

Bultmann's contention that revelation has no objective basis is open to criticism. Our concern, he says, is not with the objective-historical *(historisch)* but with the existential-historical *(geschichtlich)*. Revelation is therefore a present event, a reality in existential experience. Here again we must ask whether he does not substitute psychology for theology. Our decision of faith is important, but it can only be made on the basis of the prior decision that God has made for us in Jesus Christ.

Bultmann's tendency to separate the Christ of faith from the Jesus of history is also disconcerting. Here we can see traces of Nestorianism and even docetism. The object of faith becomes in his system the kerygma rather than the historic Jesus Christ. This is to say that he dehistoricizes as well as demythologizes.[12]

His stress on the continuity between authentic and inauthentic existence can also be questioned, for this presupposes a convergence of philosophical and theological interpretation. It also tends to deny the radical character of the new life in Jesus Christ. He has written: "Justification by faith is not demonstrable in human existence, for the justified is righteous only with God and always only with God and is a sinner on earth."[13] The new birth is new knowledge rather than a new existence for Bultmann. It signifies a new understanding of the self rather than a new self. In his theology the new life is not a quality in the human soul but the assurance of forgiveness; it is not the indwelling of the Spirit but an openness toward others. Here one can discern Bultmann's almost violent reaction against the mysticism of Herrmann and Schleiermacher.

This stress on continuity is the basis for his apologetics. Bultmann maintains that the natural man can know his lostness. He can also perceive the possibility of faith although he cannot transmute this possibility into a reality. All men have the possibility of being made alive in Christ, but this does not become a reality in their lives until they make contact with the kerygma as it is proclaimed in the Christian community. Barth argues that Bultmann makes the problem of translation the central concern in theology rather than the message of faith itself. Bultmann is consequently to be understood as a kerygmatic apologist and not as a biblical kerygmatic theologian.

Bultmann also fails to do justice to the transcendence of God. He posits a transcendence within immanence. God is "the beyond in the here" and "the unconditional in the conditional." [14] He affirms this world as God's world but denies the miraculous creation out of nothing. God confronts us in the existential experience of the cross, and therefore the only God we can speak of is a trans-subjecttive power within human experience.

Bultmann can also be criticized for not giving sufficient attention to the Old Testament. He sees the Old Testament as a pre-understanding of faith and not as an integral part of the message of faith. He has consequently been accused of Marcionism, although somewhat unjustly. Even so, he will not affirm the creation of the world by God. He has made the following statement: "For the Christian faith the Old Testament is no longer revelation as it was and is for the Jew. For him who stands in the church the history of Israel is past and done with." [15]

I can appreciate Bultmann's concern to safeguard the subjective pole of salvation, the indispensability of faith for authentic existence. I can also share to a certain degree his understanding of faith as a venture in the darkness, a venture which excludes all rational and empirical supports or securities (although we hold that faith is anchored in divinely-revealed truth). But must we not affirm *solus Christus* (Christ alone) as well as *sola fide* (faith alone)? Bultmann holds with Luther that salvation derives from the Christ preached in the church and received in repentance and faith. Yet did not something happen objectively in the death and resurrection of Jesus Christ which benefits all men even apart from faith? [16]

Finally, I take exception to Bultmann's contention that man cannot have an objective or conceptual knowledge of God. He maintains that revelation gives to man a new self-understanding but not actual knowledge concerning the being, will, and purpose of God. In his theology "statements about God and His activity" are to be understood as "statements about human existence." He contends that man cannot objectify God, because God would then be within the power and control of man. But Bultmann does not allow for the fact that God can objectify himself and that he does so whenever men are confronted by the biblical witness to Jesus Christ. God is not an object at man's disposal, but God can and does make himself available to man by his Spirit. Moreover, God also illumines the understanding of men so that they can know that he exists and also what his purpose and will are for their lives. Reason cannot grasp the meaning of revelation, but reason by the power of the Spirit can surely receive this meaning even though not fully assimilating it.

For Bultmann the only criterion is the revelatory event itself as it takes effect in human experience. For evangelical theology the criterion is not only the event but also the biblical interpretation of this event. Existentialist theology is guilty of abstracting the revelatory event from the biblical witness. What Bultmann lacks is confidence in the Bible as the authentic and definitive witness to the revelation of God.

VI.
Reinhold Niebuhr

Reinhold Niebuhr was a pastor in an Evangelical Lutheran church in Detroit, Michigan, for 13 years before becoming a professor in the field of Applied Christianity at Union Theological Seminary in 1928.[1] His basic concern has been to establish the eternal relevance of the Christian faith to a secularized and disillusioned culture. At the same time he has sought to eschew the errors of the early apologists which resulted in a biblical-classical synthesis as well as the errors of Protestant liberalism which transmuted biblical faith into either an idealistic or naturalistic philosophy of religion. Niebuhr has exerted a profound influence not only upon the religious thought of our time but also upon modern secular and political thought.

In his earlier years Niebuhr was very much influenced by the Social Gospel movement; he even espoused the cause of pacifism. He later abandoned liberalism and pacifism, but he has retained his intense social concern. He has been active in both the Socialist and Liberal parties and was a fervent supporter of Franklin Roosevelt's New Deal. He was the founder of the politically perceptive magazine *Christianity and Crisis,* which seeks to relate the Gospel to the critical issues of our time.

His first book, *Does Civilization Need Religion?* (1927), represents the liberal stage of his career. Here he speaks of religion rather than Christianity and of religious experience rather than revelation. He states that reverence for personality is the end of action in religion. He also regards love understood as a social force as the hope of society. At the same time, Niebuhr is realistic enough to discern that men's moral achievements are not exempt from cultural conditioning and self-regard. He also candidly acknowledges that liberal Christianity, by adjusting itself to the ethos of this age, destroyed "the sense of depth and the experience of tension, typical of profound religion." [2]

The concern that has gripped him throughout his career has been the ethical imperatives of the faith. He was strengthened in this concern by the callous exploitation of its working men by the Ford Industry of Detroit. Even in his earliest writings he contends that the irreligious mood of our times is to be attributed to the social impotence of religion and not so much to intellectual difficulties. It is the seeming irrelevance of Christian teaching and not the incredibility of the biblical message that accounts for much of the unbelief of our times. He became deeply critical of abstractionism in preaching. He declared: "The average man is not disturbed when convicted of selfishness as long as he is not told how, when and where he is selfish and his actions are not set in the light of specific alternatives." [3]

Niebuhr is noted for his penetrating critique of liberal Protestantism. Even in his book *Does Civilization Need Religion?* the ethic of liberal theology is charged with being individualistic and colored by the religious needs of the privileged classes. In his *Reflections on the End of an Era* and *Moral Man and Immoral Society* he becomes increasingly pessimistic concerning the moral capabilities of man and the general health of western culture.

Marxist ideas are dominant in his interpretation of society. He now speaks of the class struggle and of an ideological taint in human reasoning. He holds that peace can be maintained only by a balance of egoisms. The only peace that we can know in this life is either an uneasy armistice or a Roman peace. His break with pacifism is marked by his contention that it is not violence that is intrinsically immoral but only ill-will. The way of the cross, he writes, is nonresistance, not nonviolent resistance. In his *Moral Man and Immoral Society* he demonstrates the impossibility of carrying through an absolute ethic in society.

In his *An Interpretation of Christian Ethics* (1935) Niebuhr holds that the ideal of love is relevant but not possible. The love of God is a goal and norm but not a simple possibility even for a Christian. We are judged but not saved by love. There is no place in history where the ideal of love has been realized in pure form. Love can only appear in history as suffering love; sacrificial love was manifested in Jesus Christ to a supreme degree in the crucifixion, an event which stands at the edge of history. Such love enters into history, but it does not arise out of history.

Niebuhr affirms the Saviorhood of Jesus but not his deity. The Gospel is the revelation of God's love in Christ, but nothing is said of a perfect sacrifice for sin performed by Jesus as a man. It is what God does in Jesus that is regarded as decisive. Here one can discern a tendency to Nestorianism and even docetism in Niebuhr's theology.

In his *Beyond Tragedy* (1937) his emphasis is on Christ as a historical revelation. He is adamant in his contention that the Christian revelation occurred in history, but he holds that the biblical witness to revelation is highly symbolic. He can even refer to Christ as a symbol, but he means by it that the historical Christ mirrors the moral ideal. He maintains that we must take the mythical symbolism of the Bible seriously but not literally.[4] In the same year he distinguishes between pre-scientific or primitive myths and permanent myths.[5] The myth of the fall of Adam is viewed as one that has permanent validity.

In his monumental *The Nature and Destiny of Man* Niebuhr outlines his anthropology. He points to the predicament of man and to the final answer to man's dilemma in the cross of Christ. The predicament of man is not his bestial heritage nor ignorance but rather original sin. The occasion for sin is man's anxiety over his finitude; the possibility of sin is located in the freedom of man to transcend himself. Man is tempted either to deny the contingent character of his existence (in pride) or to escape from the responsibilities of his freedom (in sensuality). Sin is inevitable, but it is not a necessary implication of man's nature. He recognizes, however, that anxiety over finitude would not be sufficient to induce man to sin unless sin were already in the picture. Whereas pride is the religious dimension of sin, injustice represents the social dimension. Collective pride is the worst form of sin.

Niebuhr seeks a synthesis of Renaissance and Reformation insights into the plight and redemption of man. The Renaissance emphasized the indeterminate possibilities of man, and the Reformation placed the accent on man's corruption and depravity. Man is not totally depraved, Niebuhr maintains, since he still has the freedom to choose or deny the good; yet every choice that man makes is marred by self-interest and therefore is morally wanting. Salvation consists in the knowledge of God's forgiveness assured to man in the sacrificial death of Jesus on the cross. Such knowledge liberates man from care and fear, and yet it does not insure him against suffering and temptation. Faith is a having and a not having. We are saved not in the sense that we are made righteous but that we are directed toward the righteousness of Christ, which will finally triumph in the end. The church itself is never free from idolatrous presumption. The hope of man lies in the resurrection of the dead and in the kingdom of God beyond history.

Niebuhr's theology is essentially apologetic. His concern is to demonstrate the relevance of the faith to a secular culture. Apologetics is possible, he maintains, because of general revelation. "Without the private revelation of God, the public and historical revelation would not gain credence."[6] Moreover, there is a continuity between the human *nous* (mind) and the divine *logos,* the human spirit and the Holy Spirit. Therefore man can recognize the Word of God when it is addressed to him. Yet Niebuhr is also aware of the discontinuity between God and man. He has declared: "There is enough natural grace in the human heart to respond to the challenge of the real message of the gospel—and enough original sin in human nature to create opposition to it." [7] He accuses Roman Catholic theology of trying to explicate the faith rationally "in such a way that mystery is too simply resolved into ostensible rational intelligibility." [8] Liberal apologetics erred in regarding the truth of faith as capable of simple correlation with any system of rational coherence. For Niebuhr, revelation stands against the wisdom and achievements of the world. He attacks fundamentalism for seeking to prove the Gospel by appealing to miraculous validation, but he also opposes Barthianism, which tends to abandon the apologetic task altogether. We must not isolate ourselves from the cultural debate but enter into it.

Niebuhr acknowledges that we cannot make faith rationally compelling, but insists that we can demonstrate its relevance to secular man. One way of doing this is to point to the inadequacies of alternative positions. Another way is to show how the Christian faith answers the creative questions of the culture.[9] The mood of despair which characterizes the modern world is the soil out of which faith can grow. Yet Niebuhr distinguishes between a defiant despair which issues in rebellion and the "creative despair" that induces faith.[10] The point of contact according to Niebuhr is the universal consciousness of guilt; by puncturing the idolatries of man and unmasking the illusions in his life we can open the door to his recognition of the abiding truth of the Gospel. Niebuhr maintains that reason both precedes and follows faith. Once faith is accepted then it validates itself by making sense out of life.

His norm is both objective and subjective, transcendent and immanent. It consists in the paradoxical unity of the meaning of the cross and an enlightened reason or conscience. The absolute criterion is sometimes spoken of as the mind of Christ and also as the *agape* of Christ. This absolute, spiritual norm, however, is not within the grasp of man; all human interpretations and formulations of the meaning of the cross are relative and provisional. Our knowledge is forever fragmentary and broken. As a result, we are compelled to walk by faith and not by sight.

Niebuhr says that revelation must not be accepted blindly. It must be weighed and measured before the bar of experience. It cannot be proved, but its claim can be validated. It can be validated negatively by pointing to the limits of historic forms of wisdom and virtue. It can be validated positively by showing how it illumines the totality of human experience. The most potent validation of revelation is to be found in carefree and victorious lives. Christianity can be shown to be true because of the lives of its saints. Here again one can discern Niebuhr's concern for the moral life.

Niebuhr's theology can rightly be termed a "dialectical theology." It is oriented about the ongoing dialogue between God and man manifested to a supreme degree in Jesus Christ. This dialogue, he maintains, is obscured by ontological categories; God is not simply the ground of being or a first cause but a living personal spirit. God stands above and beyond the processes of nature and history. Faith, then, is not an ecstatic transcending of self and a touching of mystery but rather trust and decision, the result of a personal encounter. Niebuhr, therefore, is closer to Brunner than to Tillich. He stands apart from Barth, however, in that he holds that this dialogue is between God and the natural man and not exclusively between God and the new man in Christ.

A particularly appropriate term for Niebuhr's theology, one which he himself readily accepts, is "Christian realism." It can be called "realistic" because it seeks to take seriously the harsh realities of the human situation illumined by biblical faith.[11] Such a theology is to be contrasted with every form of perfectionism and idealism. It is provisionally pessimistic because it discerns that all human ventures and accomplishments are tainted by individual and collective pride. Yet it is ultimately optimistic in that it acknowledges the final cosmic triumph of the grace of God at the end of time.

* * * * *

Niebuhr maintains that the Christian witness in a secular age should consist of a prophetic criticism of the idolatry in society. His sermons, as a result, are basically apologetic in orientation; in them he seeks to show the limitations of reason and to point to the wisdom of the cross that alone makes sense of the contradictions and ambiguities in human existence. His sermons are based on biblical texts but cannot be considered expository nor kerygmatic. He seeks to conjoin the biblical text and man's existential predicament. He often alludes to the forgiving grace of God or the cross of Christ at the conclusion of his sermons.

There is a danger in Niebuhr's approach. The danger is that we shall preach a point of view rather than the Gospel of Christ. Niebuhr himself seeks to validate the biblical perspective rather than proclaim the Christian message in a direct manner.[12] He has compared his role to that of Schleiermacher in his addresses to the cultured despisers of religion. Niebuhr's method has convinced many agnostics of the credibility of the Christian view of man, but they generally remain agnostic concerning the saving work of Christ. Many of his hearers will accept the Christian understanding of sin and even the possibility of the existence of God, but they will not commit themselves to the living Christ. Thus has been born the phrase "the atheist followers of Niebuhr."

It is doubtful whether Niebuhr takes seriously enough the sinful corruption of natural reason. He has criticized Catholic apologists and modernists for exempting reason from the stain of sin, yet he continues to speak of a point of contact between reason and revelation. The point of contact is man's uneasy conscience. He declares that "faith in Christ could find no lodging place in the human soul, were it not uneasy about the contrast between its true and its present state; though this same faith in Christ also clarifies that contrast." [13] He tries to combine natural theology and a theology of revelation. His starting point is the self-transcending spirit of man rather than the incarnation of God in Jesus Christ. At the same time it must be recognized that Niebuhr seeks to affirm the mystery of the incarnation, and he does delineate his anthropology in the light of the biblical revelation.

Niebuhr has often been criticized for not giving sufficient attention to the divine sanctification of man. He has written that we are redeemed in principle but not in fact, that we are saved only by hope. Here he follows the Protestant Reformation in picturing justification as primarily an extrinsic forensic act by which man is accounted righteous even though he remains in sin. At the same time there are passages in his works which point to the daily sanctification and purification of man the sinner. It cannot be gainsaid that he acknowledges not only the grace of God toward man but also divine grace in man. Still his emphasis is much more on the forgiveness of sins than on the new life in Christ. Love represents not an "immediate possibility" but an "ultimate possibility" even for the Christian. Niebuhr frequently calls it an "impossible possibility." The Christian is always in a state of sin as well as in a state of grace, and his conversion from the old life is therefore only a beginning. The fact that Niebuhr nevertheless points to the Christian life as the only final validation of faith proves that he does have a doctrine of sanctification and that this doctrine is much more important in his theology than it might at first appear to be. Niebuhr's emphasis is on man the sinner, yet he opens the doorway to a theology of sainthood which he did not take time to develop.

Niebuhr has referred to the Christ event as the final revelation, the ultimate norm by which we measure all private revelations. In this event "the whole meaning of history" is disclosed.[14] Nevertheless, what is revealed is not a definitive Word from the beyond but rather the power of suffering love which was fully present in Jesus and victorious even in his death. Niebuhr refuses to speak of the revelation of Christ as "absolute truth." [15] Instead he affirms that in the cross of Christ there was a "significant disclosure of divine judgment and mercy." The cross is normative only because it symbolizes the perfection of *agape*. In his theology the final dyke against relativism is not the biblical message of salvation but rather the law of love; this, moreover, is a norm which is not superimposed upon man from above but rather one that is universally experienced.[16] The cross of Christ is the perfect embodiment of this norm, fully illumining and clarifying it. That Niebuhr actually looks beyond the cross as a historical event in arriving at his final criterion can be seen in the fact that he distinguishes the children of light from the children of darkness on the basis of a commitment to social righteousness and not on the basis of faith in Jesus Christ as the Savior from sin.[17]

The logic of his theology prevents him from giving full assent to the church's confession of Jesus Christ as the God-Man, a person whose origin lies ultimately in God and not in sinful humanity. Niebuhr is equivocal in this area, and yet it would seem that for him Jesus is a prophetic figure who was totally possessed by divine love rather than a divine person who had assumed human nature. Like Bultmann and Brunner he denies the Virgin Birth of Jesus and also his bodily resurrection from the grave. He also refuses to affirm the sinlessness of Jesus. Alan Richardson maintains that Niebuhr never succeeds in uniting the Jesus of history and the Christ of faith, so that the latter becomes nonhistorical.[18]

Niebuhr has made a lasting contribution to Christian theology in his perception of the paradox and mystery in the Christian faith. He admirably seeks to hold together both the objective and subjective poles of salvation and revelation. He endeavors to hold in paradoxical tension both divine grace and human free will. He is also to be greatly appreciated for his cogent analysis of the sinful predicament of man. He rightly points to the fact that sin is rooted not only in the individual man but also in the social matrix in which men find themselves. His original contribution is in unmasking the collective dimensions of sin. Yet the question can be asked as to whether he perceives the full extent of man's bondage to sin, since he holds that the natural man is capable of discovering his bondage. This capability, Niebuhr contends, is the ultimate proof of man's freedom; but I question whether man has the freedom to know himself, even his misery, apart from divine revelation.

Niebuhr also is to be given credit for maintaining the eschatological dimension of the Christian faith. He sees the coming of Christ in triumph as both the *finis* and *telos* of history. The kingdom of God, he maintains, is a gift and not an achievement of man. The kingdom is always coming, but it is never in fact here. It impinges upon history but will never be realized within history. The blessedness of this future kingdom can be experienced now through the power of the Holy Spirit, but the kingdom of God lies essentially "beyond history." We can always make progress toward this goal, but we can never attain it within the sphere of earthly history. Here Niebuhr is to be contrasted with Barth, who maintains that the kingdom has already been realized and that all that remains is the revelation of this fact to the world.

Lastly, Niebuhr can be appreciated because he acutely discerns the social relevance of the Gospel. His criticisms of the moral pessimism and cultural indifferentism of the Reformation are well made. His strictures on the perfectionism of pietistic Evangelicalism and Roman Catholicism are also very sound. Niebuhr rightly discerns that individual conversion cannot by itself bring about the moral rejuvenation of society. He has written against contemporary mass evangelism: "Individual conversion . . . can deal only with the moral corruptions which violate a general standard. It has never been successful in correcting the standard." [19] He also recognizes that the ideal of love as proclaimed in the circles of liberal Protestantism cannot be regarded as a practical remedy for the ills of the world. He insists that love must be combined with justice. Conversion must be conjoined with social action. For Niebuhr, the hopes for a better world lie in a redemptive community, not merely in redeemed individuals. These hopes, however, must remain relative and transitory. Not even a reformed and purified Christian church, not even a world federation of nations, can assure men that their dreams for a new life will be realized. The ultimate hope of the Christian lies not in any earthly institution but rather in the coming kingdom of God.

VII.
Paul Tillich

Paul Tillich was for many years a professor of systematic theology at Union Seminary in New York. Before that time he had taught theology at various universities in Germany. When the Nazis assumed power he was forced to seek employment outside his homeland, partly because of his activities in the religious socialist movement. After his retirement from Union he taught at the Harvard Divinity School and the Divinity School of the University of Chicago. Tillich's influence is perhaps more far-reaching upon the contemporary world of political, social, and theological thought than that of any other theologian in our study.

Tillich has a pessimistic view concerning the future of Protestantism. He does not hesitate to speak of the present "post-Protestant era," by which he means that Protestantism has ceased to have formative influence in contemporary culture. Protestant religion has become too closely identified with bourgeois culture and the emerging nationalism. He contends:

> Protestantism as a church for the masses can continue to exist only if it succeeds in undergoing a fundamental change. To do this it must obtain a new understanding of symbols and all those things which we have called "sacred objectivities." To continue to live, it must reformulate its appeal so that it will provide a message which a disintegrated world seeking reintegration will accept.[1]

The demise of Protestantism is closely related to the rise of secularism, which Tillich does not categorically condemn. Insofar as secularism means the protest against religious authoritarianism and fanaticism for the sake of a relative autonomy in the areas of the common life, then it can certainly be welcomed. On the other hand, secularism also means the loss of an ultimate concern and thereby prepares the way for spiritual emptiness and finally the absolutizing of finite realities.

The anxiety of meaninglessness, which he maintains is the curse of the modern age, is to be attributed to secularization, or what he also calls profanization. Tillich points to the cause of the spiritual sickness in modern life: "The spiritual disintegration of our day consists in the loss of an ultimate meaning of life by the people of Western civilization. And with the loss of the meaning of life, they have lost personality and community." [2]

Tillich maintains that the Christian message must be made concrete and contemporaneous. It must be related to the existential situation in which men find themselves. It must be expressed in new categories and thought forms. At the same time the symbols of the faith should not be abandoned but rather reinterpreted.

> . . . my whole theological work has been directed precisely to the interpretation of religious symbols in such a way that the secular man—and we are all secular—can understand and be moved by them.[3]

He called his theology "belief-ful realism," "self-transcending realism," "self-transcending naturalism," "ecstatic naturalism," and "eschatological panentheism." His position has also been termed "neosupernaturalism" because he speaks of the infinite distance between God and man and the necessity for divine revelation.

Tillich, though, declares himself against supernaturalism. He refuses to acknowledge an order of existence that transcends the natural order. There is no transcendent or heavenly world above our world, he maintains. God is not a divine person who dwells in the highest heaven; rather he is the ground of being and the depth of selfhood. Everything we say concerning God is symbolic. A symbol, according to Tillich, participates in the reality to which it points. Symbols provide "no objective knowledge" but rather "a true awareness" of the mystery of the ground of being.[4] The only non-symbolic statement we can make about God is that he is Being-itself.

Tillich contrasts his approach, which he labels "theonomy," meaning authority centered in God, with autonomy (self-centered authority) and heteronomy (which locates authority in an external standard or institution). The absolute standpoint, Tillich maintains, cannot be possessed; it can only be expressed in symbolic, paradoxical statements. The safeguard of theonomous religion is "the Protestant principle" which he defines as the divine and human protest against any absolute claim made for a relative or finite reality.

Absolute faith, according to Tillich, transcends the divine-human encounter. This faith is devoid of any special content, yet it has a content which might be described as "the God above God." Christian faith posits a God who transcends the God of theism; such a God does not exist, since he transcends even existence. There is personality in God, but God is not a person; rather God is the ground of personality. This God transcends mysticism, for mystical experience can make contact with him but cannot possess him.

Faith is an ecstatic state of being grasped by the presence of God. In faith the subject-object relationship is surmounted. God is no longer an object in the experience of faith but a Subject. Still he is not a Subject apart from us but the Subject within and beyond all spaces and times. He is the ground of both objectivity and subjectivity. The knowledge of faith is a receiving but not a controlling knowledge; it can be regarded as ecstatic rather than objective knowledge. The truth of faith is existential rather than scientific truth.

Tillich maintains that all men experience the Spiritual Presence. This experience is sometimes spoken of as a "phenomenological intuition" of the Unconditioned. In his *Systematic Theology* he speaks of the "mystical apriori," the immediate awareness of the divine power which all men have to a certain degree. But this universal mystical experience must be related to the historical norm, Jesus Christ. Our individual revelations must be measured by the final revelation if we are to gain spiritual wisdom and inner freedom. Jesus Christ is the criterion and goal of all private revelations. He is "the concrete absolute," the New Being, the Word of God. The Christ event signifies the absolute *kairos,* the fulfillment of time.

Yet Tillich insists that the Word of God is manifest not only in Jesus but in every charismatic personality, even in holy places and things. Anything can become transparent to the ground of being. Anything can become a symbol of the Word of God. The whole world is potentially sacramental.

Salvation signifies restoration and reunion with the ground of being. The fall of man consists in an estrangement from his true self and from the ground of selfhood. Anxiety and guilt are the consequences of this estrangement. Tillich does not adhere to a historical fall, but he speaks of an immanent or psychological fall and a transcendent fall (the point where creation and disruption coincide). Salvation means our acceptance by God (which is revealed in Jesus Christ) and also transformation by his Spirit. We are accepted despite the fact that we are unacceptable; this is how Tillich reinterprets the doctrine of *sola gratia.* The consummation of salvation is eternal life, participation in the kingdom of God. Tillich does not hold to self-conscious immortality in a supernatural heaven; instead he speaks of the fulfillment of selfhood and reunion with Godhead.

Tillich calls his theology apologetic rather than kerygmatic. It is philosophical rather than confessional, dialectical and not neo-orthodox. In dialectical theology, according to Tillich, the question of God is a human possibility. Barth's theology is not dialectical, he argues, since Barth denies that natural man can ask about God.[5]

In apologetic theology we enter the cultural situation in order to correlate the creative questions of the culture with the Christian answer. Tillich sees his theology as a mediating theology, one that mediates between the message and the culture, the *theos* and the *logos,* mystery and wisdom. It is also an answering theology, for it seeks to answer the questions implied in the generally human and historical situation. He maintains that secular philosophy is able to ask the truly profound questions concerning the problem of being because natural man is in quest of the New Being. Tillich therefore sees a place for both natural theology and the philosophy of religion. He seeks, however, a new role for these disciplines: "What we formerly called natural theology and the philosophy of religion should be transformed into an analysis of the questions implied in the structure of human existence and existence generally." [6]

Apologetics presupposes common ground with secular thought, a mutually acknowledged criterion. Tillich holds that this common ground is the universal estrangement from being. All men experience the "ontological shock," an existential anxiety concerning their finitude. The answer to man's anxiety is the "courage to be," a courage created by the Spiritual Presence. This is the courage to accept the fact that we have been accepted by the Power above all earthly powers. It means to accept our anxiety and to bear it.

Tillich maintains that in this secular age there can be no direct proclamation of the Christian message. Modern man cannot accept miracles. This does not mean, however, that we should abandon the mythical form of the message. Indeed, he says that we must speak in pictures and symbols in making clear the power of the New Being.

Our witness should take a threefold form, he believes. First, "it must destroy the secret reservations harbored by the modern man which prevent him from accepting resolutely the limits of his existence." [7] Secondly, it must pronounce the "yes" that comes to man in the boundary situation. Finally, it must herald the reality of the New Being through which alone it is able to say its word in power. This does not mean, though, that we are to preach Christianity; rather, we should direct men to the New Being which is the norm and judge of Christianity as of all other religions. The New Being appeared in Jesus to a superlative degree, but this reality has also appeared in charismatic and prophetic figures in every religion and in all times.

To communicate the message of the New Being means to put it before people so that they are able to decide for or against it. Here one can discern a marked difference between Tillich and Karl Barth, who contends that true freedom means only the possibility of obedience. Tillich's sermons are oriented about the call to existential decision. In freedom we have lost Paradise; in freedom we can regain it. To be sure, our freedom is grounded in grace, and yet grace empowers us to make use of our freedom and to receive the New Being into our lives.

Tillich reminds us that our witness is partly conditioned by the culture in which we live. He affirms an absolute norm, but we have this norm only in a message that is partly relative and in formulations that are ever changing. We must acknowledge the relativity of the Christian message and yet affirm that its ground is absolute and ultimate.

* * * * *

The first part of our critique concerns Tillich's reappraisal of the doctrine of God. Tillich's "ground of being" seems a far cry from the living personal God of the Bible who enters into dialogue with his creatures. To be sure, Tillich's God contains both personal and impersonal elements—he even calls God "transpersonal"—but does this mean that there are areas of the personality of God that remain hidden, or that God is beyond personality? Tillich seems to imply the latter, but a God who is beyond personality is less than and not more than personal. The God of the Bible transcends the humanly personal, but only because he is the divinely personal, not an impersonal or transpersonal ground of being. The fact that Tillich has no real place for petitionary prayer in his system is a sign that his God is other than personal. Tillich's idea of transcendence proves to be actually a higher form of immanence (after the pattern of Hegel). It is a transcendence within immanence, and therefore the Tillichian term "self-transcending naturalism" would seem to be an appropriate designation for his theology.

Tillich acknowledges Jesus Christ as a final and unique revelation of God, and yet he refuses to affirm the hypostatic union of the divine and human natures in Christ. He speaks of Jesus as the Christ, but he will not speak of Jesus Christ as God. He affirms not that God became man but rather that God has manifested himself through man. He therefore tends to separate the Christ of faith from the Jesus of history. He even contends that it is possible to make a decision for Christ without knowing about Jesus.[8] What is decisive is only whether men act for or against the law of love which was manifested in Jesus. Tillich has even declared that the historical existence of Jesus is not absolutely necessary for faith.[9]

Tillich also tends to separate the Christ event from the Christian religion. At first glance he appears to stand squarely within the Christian tradition; he affirms the authority of the biblical witness, the revelation of vicarious love in Jesus Christ, salvation by grace, and justification by faith alone. Yet the grace and love of Christ are also believed to be manifest in other religions to some degree, so that the ultimate criterion is not the Christian faith but the power of the New Being which is universal in its scope and outreach. Can Tillich avoid a kind of eclecticism which seeks to include insights from all religions? When he affirms that self-discovery is tantamount to God-discovery it would seem that he is much closer to Hinduism than to classical Christianity.

This brings us to Tillich's method of correlation. Robert Johnson holds that this methodology verges toward the coalescence of theology and philosophy and thereby severely compromises the integrity of the faith.[10] It would seem that Tillich allows the culture to dictate not only the questions but also the formulations and even the content of the Christian answer. He admits that his theology is a philosophical rather than a strictly biblical theology. His high doctrine of grace prevents him from succumbing to secular philosophy. Yet it cannot be denied that Neo-Platonic mysticism, the mysticism of Jacob Boehme, the idealistic philosophy of Hegel, and the existentialism of Heidegger, play a determinative role in his system. The distinction which Tillich sometimes makes between God and Being-itself, or between God in his self-manifestation and God in his abysmal nature, bears a marked resemblance to Plotinus' distinction between Divine Reason and the One and Meister Eckhart's distinction between God and the Godhead. Tillich's practical equation of existence and estrangement reflects the Platonic notion that finite existence is defective. The Tillichian terms "ground" and "abyss" are derived from Boehme.[11]

Tillich's apologetics is based on the supposed quest of reason for relevation, since revelation effects the reintegration of reason.[12] But if the reason of the natural man is subservient to his self-seeking will, can we speak of a quest of reason for God? In Romans 3, Paul reaffirms the Old Testament belief that no man seeks for God. The deeper biblical insight of the estrangement in reason itself breaks through only on rare occasions in Tillich's sermons.[13] Barth is more sound in this respect than Tillich when he says: "Who on his own initiative can seek and ask for the God of whose mercy the Gospel speaks?"[14]

Tillich, like Brunner and Niebuhr, sees contrite despair as the absolute prerequisite for a living and dynamic faith. He states that the duty of the preacher is to drive men to the "boundary situation" so that they can make the leap of faith. Here he follows a traditional Lutheran view that despair leads to repentance and the law leads to the Gospel. But can we really despair of ourselves until we see ourselves in the light of the cross of Jesus Christ? Tillich holds after the manner of Niebuhr and Bultmann that self-knowledge prepares the way for God-knowledge. But can we know ourselves as we really are until we have been awakened to the infinite compassion and gracious election of God as revealed in Jesus Christ? Is it not from Jesus Christ himself that we derive a knowledge of our sin and of our need for salvation?[15]

It is Tillich's view that the experience of estrangement is the tie that links Christians and non-Christians. This common experience makes the apologetic task possible. But does estrangement as this is understood by the culture correspond to what the Bible means by sin? Does the anxiety of meaninglessness, which is the malady of our secular culture, correspond to the anxiety of guilt? Tillich acknowledges that these two kinds of anxiety are not identical, but he insists that they can be correlated.

According to Tillich man is alienated from the ground of his being, but he cannot be spoken of as "lost" in the sense of standing under the eternal condemnation of God. All men are in the Spiritual Community whether in its latent or manifest form. "The evangelist does not address 'lost souls,' men without God, but people in the stage of latency . . . ."[16] There can be no such thing as an absolute conversion, since all men are on the way to salvation. But we can speak, he says, of "relative conversions," which means bringing men to a conscious commitment to the New Being.

Tillich can be appreciated for his effort to keep the doorways open between theology and the disciplines of culture. He rightly discerns that when we have lost the intelligentsia we have forfeited the possibility of directing and influencing the culture. His analysis of the secularization of modern culture, particularly in *The Protestant Era,* is both profound and enlightening.

The enigma of Tillich's theology is that it seeks to be both biblical and philosophical. Despite the biblical strands in his system it would seem that biblical faith has been compromised. The self-understanding of man and not God's act of reconciliation in Christ is his point of departure. He begins not with the Gospel of the cross but with the dilemma and gropings of secular man, so that what he has given us is not theology in the classical sense but anthropology. Human existence, although a worthy subject of theological study, cannot be the starting point nor even the pivotal point of theology; the foundation of a biblical systematic theology can only be the Word of God as attested in Holy Scripture. It certainly cannot be the cultural self-interpretation or the creative questions of secular philosophy. Tillich has written: "A consequence of the method used in apologetic theology is that the concept of revelation is approached from 'below,' from man in the situation of revelation, and not from 'above,' from the divine ground of revelation."[17] Perhaps what is needed in a day when the faith itself is becoming secularized is a kerygmatic theology which confronts the cultural situation with the authoritative message of divine revelation.

VIII.
Dietrich Bonhoeffer

Perhaps no other theologian has done more to shape the contemporary theological climate than Dietrich Bonhoeffer, the German Lutheran pastor who was hanged by the Nazis in the concentration camp at Flossenburg in 1945. The new secular theology has been inspired in part by Bonhoeffer's *Letters and Papers from Prison*. His book *The Cost of Discipleship* is regarded in nearly all branches of Christendom as a modern Christian classic.

A few words should be said about his background. He was born into a cultured but not particularly pious Lutheran family, being the son of a doctor. He undertook theological study with Karl Holl and Reinhold Seeberg in Berlin. Although he never studied with Barth, he was greatly influenced by the Swiss theologian. He also did theological work at Union Theological Seminary in New York (1930-31). From the beginning of his theological career he was active in ecumenical circles. While in Berlin he lectured at the University in systematic theology, helped to found a settlement house, and also served as the chaplain at the Technical University.

His concern from the first was the quest for the concrete nature of the Christian message. In his doctoral thesis *Sanctorum Communio* (published in 1930) he seeks to relate revelation to the church. He maintains that concreteness is an attribute of revelation itself. Revelation signifies not an abstract, eternal truth but rather "an entity in this historically and sociologically shaped world." [1] It is in community that we meet Christ. Because of this, theology must be integrally related to sociology, and religion must be viewed in the context of culture.

Bonhoeffer holds that incarnation is the key to communication. The Word had to become flesh and dwell among us before we could behold his glory. Bonhoeffer does not regard the church as an extension of the incarnation of Christ, but he does maintain that Christ is incarnate in his church. It is through his members, through their deeds of service and compassion, that Christ relates himself to the world. Our message therefore must be not in words alone but in flesh and blood. Only the message which becomes a specific concrete word is the eternal word of authority.

In his *Act and Being* (published in 1931) he contends that philosophy is powerless to place man in the truth. He says: "Revelation is its own donor, without preconditions, and alone has the power to place in reality. From God to reality, not from reality to God, goes the path of theology." [2] Faith, for Bonhoeffer, is something different from religion. Religion is stimulated by man, but only God can bestow faith.

Despite his close affinity with Barth during this period Bonhoeffer is not uncritical of his mentor. In his view Barth's conception of revelation is too transcendent. He rejects the Calvinist and Barthian formula: *finitum non capax infiniti.* He maintains in contrast, that by the power of grace the finite can receive and reveal the infinite; thus he adheres to the traditional Lutheran concept of the means of grace. Again, he argues that Barth introduces reflection into faith. Reflection is loneliness and allows for abstraction; faith, on the other hand, is sociality and the experience of the concreteness of the incarnated.

The second period of Bonhoeffer's theological career is marked by his struggle with National Socialism. Now his concern is to reestablish the costly character of grace and faith. His two major works in this period are *The Cost of Discipleship (Nachfolge)* and *Life Together.* It was during this time that he supervised a Brothers' House in Pomerania which functioned as an illegal theological training center.

Bonhoeffer affirms that the only grace that saves is costly grace. This is grace that cost Jesus Christ his very life on the cross; it must also cost us our comfort and security. The bane of the modern church is "cheap grace," which is baptism without church discipline, the preaching of forgiveness without repentance, communion without confession, and absolution without contrition.

He states the case for concrete witnessing, by which he means relating ourselves and our message to the specific needs and agonies of the world about us. Concrete witnessing is none other than discipleship or "servanthood." It also entails sharing in community life or *koinonia.* The Christian family, he maintains, is the paradigm or basis for Christian community. Discipleship consists in the imitation of Jesus Christ, the bearing of the cross in service to others. It entails being *against* the spirit of the world but being *for* the lost and helpless in the world. The Christian must therefore seek *separation from* as well as *solidarity with* the world.

The main works in Bonhoeffer's third period are his *Ethics* and *Letters and Papers from Prison.* The theme in this period is Christianity without religion. He holds that the world has come of age, that is, the world has cast off every remnant of superstition and religiousness. In the secular age in which we live ultimate concerns are secondary to penultimate concerns. Men are preoccupied not with an otherworldly salvation but with such basic issues as "land, peace, and bread" (Lenin). We must believe in the ultimate, Bonhoeffer contends, but we must strive to live on the basis of the penultimate. The penultimate means life in this world. We therefore must seek to reach men not on the frontiers of life, at the limits of reason, but in the center of life, in the daily concerns of life. Our witnessing must take the form of *diakonia,* service to the outcasts and the needy. Secularism should be regarded not only as a defect but also as an ally of Christian faith, for after all, it signifies the end of idolatry and superstition. Secularism is a necessary, positive movement in God's symphony. Whereas in his first period he described the church as the real presence of Christ, Bonhoeffer now speaks of Christ's presence in terms of the stranger and refugee outside the doors of the church.

Bonhoeffer points out that discipleship entails holy worldliness. This is not to be confused with the unholy this-worldliness that characterizes the godless man, but it is also to be distinguished from the otherworldliness that has plagued pietism and revivalism. Discipleship means to be conformed to the incarnate one; it means to become truly human. Sanctity and true humanity are thereby closely allied.

Bonhoeffer, like Barth, opposes apologetics, but he takes his opposition a step further. He refuses even to engage in polemics with the world. We are not to defend ourselves, he says, but rather only to serve with compassion. We are not to utilize despair for apologetic purposes but only to minister to man in his despair by showing him that God cares. God is to be found not at the boundary of life (as Niebuhr and Tillich maintain) but rather in the midst of life. Apologetics, he contends, is ignoble because it seeks to exploit the weakness of man. It is also pointless because it does not recognize man in his maturity. The Christian is not to be a salesman but only a servant and instrument of the Word.[3]

Nevertheless, Bonhoeffer will not align himself with a kerygmatic theology. Barth's positivism of revelation, he argues, separates the Christian message from the world. What is needed is a nonreligious interpretation that establishes the relation of revelation to the world. This implies a Christian style of life rather than the mouthing of clichés or abstract preaching.

Bonhoeffer returns often to this theme of concrete witnessing, witnessing by life and work and not merely by speech. The criterion for such witnessing is not the believer but the unbeliever. This does not mean that we are to appeal to the self-understanding of natural man; rather it means that we are to concern ourselves with his needs and problems. The preaching of Christ basically entails "being Christ" to our neighbor. We should speak, but only at the right time and in the right place, and when we do so we should utilize the secular everyday language of the world and not the confessional, metaphysical language of the church. We must not seek to force our views on others; rather we must be willing to give of ourselves for the welfare of others. As one of Bonhoeffer's admirers has put it, "Jesus sends us as sheep among wolves, not to turn wolves into sheep, but to be eaten by wolves" (Vera Van Trott).

Witnessing for Christ means witnessing by suffering. He has rightly observed that our preaching of the passion cannot convince the world when we shrink from that passion in our own lives. We must also witness by prayer; the kind of evangelism which he upholds is prayer evangelism, intercession for others. He would probably oppose mass evangelism on the grounds that it tends to exploit the weaknesses of man.

Like Barth, Bonhoeffer holds that the Gospel does not need our defense. But he insists that the Gospel does demand from us our lives. We cannot accomplish the salvation of the world as did Jesus Christ on the cross, but we can reveal and communicate this salvation to others through a life under the cross.

* * * * *

It is interesting to compare Bonhoeffer with other theologians. First of all it is apparent that he has a close affinity with Kierkegaard. Kierkegaard wrestled with the problem of how to be a Christian in Christendom; both of these thinkers spoke of the perils of cheap grace and the need for costly discipleship. It is in Bonhoeffer's high doctrine of the church and the sacraments, though, that we find a marked difference between them.

Many of his theological emphases are also similar to those of Reinhold Niebuhr. Both men are concerned with specificity in witnessing, for the undergirding of witness by life; they would agree that the most telling witness today is to be found in lives of exemplary dedication. Bonhoeffer would concur with Niebuhr that we cannot preach about miracles when people see no evidence of the miraculous in our own lives.

Bonhoeffer also has a marked affinity with Barth. Both theologians affirm the revelation of Jesus Christ as the criterion and ground of theological thinking. Both seek to avoid natural theology and the philosophy of religion. But Bonhoeffer, unlike Barth, speaks not of the transcendent or pre-existent Christ but of the incarnate Christ, the Christ who meets us in the word of the sermon, in the bread and wine of the sacrament, and in the suffering and needy in the world. Bonhoeffer's is an incarnational rather than a kerygmatic theology.

He would agree with most of the theologians in our study, including Tillich and Bultmann, that a new kind of witness is needed today. But he holds, unlike some of the others, that this witness must not take the form of a demythologized Gospel or of a correlation with secular philosophy. Rather it must take the form of serving and praying and preaching born out of suffering.

The call to discipleship which Bonhoeffer sounds is surely welcome. He reminds us that witnessing *(martyria)* may imply martyrdom as well as speaking. The Reformation stress on the Word was perhaps unbalanced, but Catholic monasticism has overemphasized the role of good works in our salvation. Bonhoeffer is certainly true to Scripture in his insistence that Word and life belong together.

Bonhoeffer is not to be placed in the camp of pietistic and monastic spirituality. His emphasis is not *diastasis* (separation) but rather vicarious action. His ideal is not an exclusive fellowship, nor even a gathered community of the faithful; he sees the danger of ghettoism in the pietistic and monastic approaches. But he also does not belong to the camp of the modernists. In their attempt to relate Christian and secular values Bonhoeffer sees the peril of syncretism. His view is that the church will be in conflict with the world till the end of time; our expression of this conflict should not be in polemics against the world but in suffering in and for the world. Bonhoeffer's approach is *diakonia* rather than apologetics.

I wonder if he is on firm ground in his nonreligious interpretation of the cross. Is this really witnessing as the New Testament understands it? By a nonreligious interpretation he means first involvement with the suffering Christ and then speaking out of this involvement on concrete issues. A nonreligious approach means the eschewing of metaphysics and of a supernatural or otherworldly orientation. He does not deny the reality of the supernatural, but he questions the separation of the supernatural from the natural, the elevation of the spiritual above the temporal.[4] What he is opposed to is a preoccupation with the supernatural to the detriment of service to our neighbor in the here and now. He maintains that the concern of the Christian faith is both with life under God and life as it is lived in this world. The question remains whether he does justice to the biblical witness that this life is ephemeral and that our hope is to be placed on life in eternity.

To affirm that Jesus Christ is a heavenly Redeemer or that he is a divine person with a human as well as a divine nature is no longer tenable, according to the logic of Bonhoeffer's theology.[5] We should now speak of Christ as the suffering servant and the man for others. But can we preach Christ or even serve Christ unless we acknowledge him as a divine being who has assumed human flesh, as one who rose from the dead and ascended into heaven? To be sure, this is a religious or confessional understanding of Christ, but can this be abandoned? Bonhoeffer desires to retain the New Testament mythology as well as the biblical picture of Christ, but can this picture be maintained in the framework of a nonreligious interpretation? Unfortunately, Bonhoeffer's untimely death prevented him from working out the full implications of a Christology without religion.

Bonhoeffer in his *Letters* speaks of God in a nonreligious or secular way. He no longer refers to God as the Supreme Being but rather as "the 'beyond' in the midst of our life." [6] He maintains that modern man cannot conceive of God as a highest being, absolute in power and goodness.[7] But must not the Christian affirm God as the Creator of the world, as the personal Spirit who is not bound to this world?

Again he refers to the redemption of Christ as a *historical* redemption, one that occurs on this side of death. Yet does not Scripture speak of an *eternal* redemption (cf. 2 Cor. 4:17, 5:1, 2; Heb. 5:9, 9:12)? He also says that the kingdom of God is to be found not in the world beyond but in the very midst of this world.[8] Is not Niebuhr more sound when he declares that the kingdom of God is "beyond history"?

It must be recognized that Bonhoeffer continues to affirm the existence of God and the Saviorhood of Christ. Yet he seeks to avoid all metaphysical speculation concerning such matters. Some of his latter-day followers have gone much further in questioning the very reality of God in a secular world.

We now come to the question of whether faith can be separated from religion. In Bonhoeffer's view faith is from God, while religion is from men. The two principal characteristics of religion are metaphysical interest and inwardness.[9] Bonhoeffer holds that faith makes religion irrelevant. Barth has stated that faith overthrows religion. Reinhold Niebuhr is better here, for he sees the Christian faith as the fulfillment and negation of human religion. My position is that the man of faith will be a religious as well as a secular man; his concern will be with metaphysics as well as with ethics. The man of faith will be a mystic as well as a man of action. Indeed, can faith be divorced from mysticism as Bonhoeffer and also Barth seem to imply?

In Bonhoeffer's religionless Christianity it would seem that the sacred dimension of life has been pushed into the background. Still, Bonhoeffer will not allow it to be superseded. He continues to uphold an arcane or hidden discipline of devotion which preserves the sacred mysteries of the faith from profanization; unlike some of the new secular theologians he sees the need for holding onto the vertical or Godward dimension of life.[10]

Bonhoeffer's praise of secularism can be questioned. He has written: "The world that has come of age is more godless, and for that reason perhaps *nearer* to God, than the world as a minor was." [11] But is not secularism also a manifestation of man's rebellion against God? Bonhoeffer is not unaware of the dangers in secularism —indeed, he contrasts a "hopeless godlessness" and "a godlessness that is full of promise"—but here again Niebuhr sees the problem better. Niebuhr has maintained that secularism is a covert religion, and that its profoundest belief is that the historical process is itself redemptive and guarantees the meaning of life.[12] We must remember that the world is not only under the ultimate lordship of Christ, but it is also under the immediate rule of the powers of darkness. Bonhoeffer seems to lack a theology of the demonic in his *Letters and Papers from Prison*. In addition, his concept of a "world come of age" reflects the old secular ideology of progress. To be sure, Bonhoeffer means by this not moral but intellectual maturity. Yet can it be said that the modern age is characterized even by this kind of maturity? Technical knowledge and sophistication must not be confused with wisdom.

We can agree with Bonhoeffer that modern man is post-Christian. But is he post-religious? Bonhoeffer acknowledges the godless religion of Bolshevism, and he also discerns that Western secularism has some religious characteristics. Modern man is admittedly post-religious in the sense that he is no longer oriented toward the supernatural, and he also appears to be indifferent to the metaphysical; but is not this period of relativism abnormal? Brunner is right when he contends that the metaphysical dimensions of man's mind can never remain empty. The ultimate concern is the one concern that can move men to action; the demise of religion can only prepare the way for secular salvations which are not fully taken into account by "secular theology."

Bonhoeffer seeks to hold together two conflicting approaches to culture which H. Richard Niebuhr has termed "Christ against culture" and "Christ transforming culture." His emphasis is on the dialectic of withdrawal and return, separation and identification. But does he not revert to a third approach in the end, "Christ and culture in paradox"? This is the Lutheran dualistic strategy with which Bonhoeffer was acquainted even from his childhood days. He holds that the Christian must serve in the world but at the same time maintain a hidden discipline of worship and prayer. Here one can discern Luther's contention that the Christian lives in two kingdoms, although God is sovereign over both.

Finally, we must ask whether Bonhoeffer has not diverged from the Reformation doctrine of salvation through the free grace of God. In his *Nachfolge* he intimates that obedience can prepare the way for the gift of grace, even though he acknowledges that this obedience is a dead work of the law until it is fulfilled in repentance and faith. He also maintains that salvation is imperiled when obedience ceases (and here he has some scriptural support). In his later writings, particularly in his *Letters,* he appears to recognize the danger in seeking to procure salvation by means of a holy life, but now his emphasis is on holy worldliness. He states that only by living completely in the world can one learn to believe.[13] He is also insistent that only by living wholly for the world does one become authentically human. He affirms that "before a man can know and find Christ he must first become righteous like those who strive and who suffer for the sake of justice, truth, and humanity."[14] My question is this: Does he not come dangerously close to making the Christian life of self-giving service to others the foundation and pivotal center of our salvation? Do we begin with the disciple, or with the Savior, with the obedience of man or with the Gospel of free grace? Bonhoeffer generally succeeds in holding grace and discipleship in paradoxical relation, but some of his admirers have placed the accent on a life of outgoing love without any reference to the prior gift of grace through the vicarious sacrifice of Jesus Christ on Calvary.

IX. John Robinson

John Robinson, the Anglican Bishop of Woolwich, is among those who have called for a secular reinterpretation of the message of the faith. His purpose is to restate the Christian faith so that it can be made comprehensible and convincing to modern post-religious man. He writes: "For I want God to be as real for our modern secular scientific world as he ever was for the 'ages of faith.'" [1] What is needed, Robinson asserts, is a "theology of secularization" that takes into account the radical emancipation of modern man from religious traditions and moral codes. In contrast to Niebuhr, he maintains that a Christ is no longer expected in Western culture, and therefore our age can aptly be called "post-Christian." Robinson acknowledges that the Holy Spirit is the giver of faith, but if the Spirit is to be free to direct men's minds, "there is much mental lumber to be shifted and a deal of retranslation to be done." [2]

Robinson calls his theology a "missionary theology," since its purpose is to convince the world of the secular relevance of the Christian faith. The evangelism which he upholds is to be directed to Christians as well as non-Christians, since Christians also stand within the secular milieu. He maintains that "secular man is just as much inside the church as out of it, and just as much inside myself." [3] His theology, in other words, is for secular man, for "the man come of age." He holds that if our evangelism is to be persuasive, we must seek to dereligionize the Gospel, to express it in secular categories.

In seeking to restate the Christian witness he leans heavily on Tillich, Bonhoeffer, and Bultmann. But he does not simply repeat what these men have to say. Among the concepts which he derives from Bonhoeffer are "holy worldliness" and "religionless Christianity." Tillich has helped him to arrive at a new understanding of transcendence; he has also benefited from Tillich's observation that the loss of an ultimate concern in the modern world has afflicted men with the anxiety of meaninglessness. Bultmann's distinction between the biblical message and its mythical form has also proved very helpful.

It is difficult to place Robinson in any particular school of thought. He cannot quite be counted among the death-of-God theologians, since he affirms God as the ground of being. He maintains, however, that the God of traditional piety is dead. He has deep affinities with the school of radical biblical criticism. He can be considered one of the representatives of the "New Hermeneutic" movement along with Ebeling, R. Gregor Smith, and James Robinson. He is also associated with the current "theology of renewal," which he sharply distinguishes from a theology of restoration. He champions what he calls a "lay theology" instead of a "seminary theology." He would also wish to be placed in the camp of "ecumenical theology" and not "confessional theology."

Like Tillich, Robinson seeks to reappraise the doctrine of God in order to make it more intelligible to the secular world. He contends that we can no longer affirm the personal God of theistic religion. God is not a being beside others but the ground of being. God is to be located not in a spatial heaven but in the center of life, in the depths of existence. God and the world are not to be identified, but they must be viewed as being inseparable. This is not mysticism in the pantheistic sense but a self-transcending naturalism; God is not the deepest aspect of the self, but rather the primal source and ground of the self.

The apologetic task is possible, Robinson says, because all men experience God, even though they might not know his name. We have a positive or true experience of God when we experience ultimate reality as "Being as gracious." This common experience of "depth" in life enables us to make the concept of God once again meaningful to educated men.

It is Robinson's conviction that Jesus Christ is the supreme revelation of God. Jesus reveals God completely, but he is not God himself. Rather he is the suffering servant, "the man for others." We should speak not of his sinless perfection but of the reality of his humanity. We should concern ourselves not with his pre-existence (which is unintelligible to modern man) but with his "pro-existence," his being for others.

Robinson holds that the cross needs to be demythologized even more than the resurrection. The doctrines of the substitutionary atonement and the propitiatory sacrifice for sin are no longer tenable in modern theology; rather, the cross must be viewed as the supreme revelation of divine love. Jesus reveals to us that sin is broken not by the sacrificial propitiation of God's wrath but by participation in divine love. Man is saved when he becomes like Jesus, that is, when he gives himself for others in vicarious suffering love.

In the area of ethics Robinson maintains that love must be the only guide. Sin is to be understood not as disobedience to God but as estrangement from self and from the ground of being. It is sacrificial self-giving love that reunites us with the ground of our existence. Robinson makes it clear that code ethics, an ethics of law, must be superseded by an ethics of love. He identifies himself with the "new morality," which he contrasts with a Victorian morality that is characterized by legalism and moralism. He publicly defends D. H. Lawrence's *Lady Chatterly's Lover* as a book which likens the sex act to "holy communion." He commends the much publicized Quaker report on sex as being mature and forthright. (This report condones premarital intercourse under certain circumstances and also pleads for legal freedom for homosexuals.) He seeks to replace a "morality of obedience" with a "morality of involvement and discovery." [4] He writes: "The decisive thing in the moral judgment is not the line itself, but the presence or absence of love at the deepest level." [5] He would share Paul Lehmann's view that the goal of a Christian ethics is not morality but "maturity."

Like Bonhoeffer he advocates a "worldly holiness." Christian existence is not separated life but involved life. It signifies a life in solidarity with the world in its anguish and suffering. Liturgy is to be understood not as the rites of the church but rather as service in the world. Prayer is not an inward communion with God but simply an openness to the ground of our being and the giving of ourselves in love to our neighbor. It is not "withdrawal from the world to God" but rather "penetration through the world to God."[6] There seems to be no place in his theology for petition to a personal Lord. He shares the position of Malcolm Boyd that prayer is "not so much talking to God" as "just sharing his presence."[7] He contends that we need a nonreligious understanding of prayer—to be with and for others. It is not the interior life but the whole life that needs to be developed. He proposes a new kind of spirituality, one that begins from life rather than works toward it. In line with many other contemporary theologians he inveighs against both an ethereal mysticism and a dualistic asceticism on the grounds that they lead us away from the world. On the other hand, he defends what he calls a "secular mysticism" in which there is no longer any essential difference between ordinary life and prayer.

Robinson's eschatology is also markedly different from the traditional view. The end of the age, he maintains, is not a future crisis at the end of history but rather the victorious life and death of Jesus Christ. The second coming is none other than the gift of the Holy Spirit to the church. He also describes it as the coming of Christ into everything. The *eschaton* is Jesus Christ in the power of His Spirit, and this can be experienced ever again. He does hold to a final consummation when God will be all in all, but this will be not another coming but the working out to fulfillment of the one coming of Christ.

The church, he contends, is an instrument of the kingdom but not the kingdom itself. God works through the world as well as through the church. Indeed, our starting point should be not the church understood as the elect people of God but rather the "family of man." His theology, consequently, is not a "church dogmatics" but a secular apologetics.

In Robinson's theology evangelism consists not so much in the preaching of the reconciliation of God in Christ as in the work of reconciling men to one another. The goal of evangelism is not the conversion of "lost souls" but the socializing and humanizing of broken and alienated men; it is introducing men to a new social environment. The missionary must be concerned with civilizing as well as evangelizing in the narrow sense because the new society to which Christ calls us is a new social order in which the sacred and secular are united in an enduring synthesis.

* * * * *

Robinson seeks to restate the Gospel so that it can be made intelligible and also acceptable to secularized post-Christian man. He contends that there is a need for a "secular reinterpretation" of the Gospel "which would permit man today to be a Christian without forcing him to feel that in order to do so he must go back upon the age to which he belongs and embrace the equivalent of a 'medieval' world-view." [8] The Gospel which Robinson presents is geared to the ethos of the modern age and consequently is one that is not only demythologized but also secularized.

It must be acknowledged that Robinson performs a signal service in pointing us beyond the God of philosophical theism. Martin Marty has written: "The non-religious interpreters, like Robinson, are doing to the 'natural' (theist) background of the Gospel what the Barthians did to the 'natural' background of the Law." [9] But Robinson brings us not the living God of the Bible who towers above nature and history but only an impersonal or transpersonal God who stands in basic continuity with the cosmic order.

Robinson's theology must be understood as a reaction against the "churchiness" and insularized religion that characterize so much of modern Anglicanism. It also can be seen as an attempt to come to terms with the secularization of English church life and culture. His theology marks a fresh approach to liturgy in that he seeks to relate it to life in the world. As a consequence he is compelled to reinterpret archaic Christian symbols. His concern is not primarily esthetic but theological and ethical in that he sees worship as a means to Christian service in the world.

Robinson's attempt to restate the Christian witness, however, is undercut by his denial of the supernatural element in religion. He tends to reduce the content of the faith to what can be experienced. The resurrection, for example, signifies for him not an objective event in world history but a present experience of the victorious power of love. Like Bultmann he substitutes anthropology for theology, the experience of man for the objective work of God in

Jesus Christ. He even acknowledges that Feuerbach is right in seeking to translate theology into anthropology.[10] Here one can discern a marked difference between Robinson and Barth.

We must ask whether Robinson has a living God. Like Tillich he describes God as transpersonal. We can accept this term if it means that God is supremely personal. We acknowledge that God is not simply "a person"; rather he is *the* Person who is himself the ground and center of all personhood. By conceiving of prayer in terms other than conversation and intercession it would seem that Robinson woefully lacks a personal God.

A case could be made for the contention that Robinson abandons the Christian myth for the myth of cultural religion. C. S. Lewis makes the trenchant observation that Robinson substitutes the myth of the Earth Mother for that of the Sky Father.[11] We would maintain that the real God can be found neither in the depths of man's existence nor in the heights of man's imagination. The God of the Bible exists outside the reach of man's cognition, even outside all spaces and times. Since the publication of *Honest to God* Robinson has generally avoided the use of the term "ground of being," but he continues to affirm that God is essentially immanent and not transcendent.

In his book *Exploration into God* Robinson defends what he calls panentheism as over against theism and pantheism.[12] In panentheism every part of the universe exists in God, but his reality is more than the universe. All things are in God, and God is in all things, but God is not identical with all things. He believes that this conception is able to do justice to both the transcendence of God and the personal dimension of God's activity. In this view God and the world are interdependent rather than God being sovereign over the world. It is well to note that he cannot bring himself to affirm God as the Creator of the world. Instead he speaks of the lure of divine love which directs the evolution of the cosmic process to the level of personal response. Immanence is the form and field of transcendence; the unconditional is essentially within rather than beyond the conditional. It is difficult to ascertain whether this is actually a form of naturalistic mysticism in which God becomes the spirit or soul of the world. He speaks of God as the personal center of all things, but he cannot envisage God as a divine person.

In panentheism God operates in and through personality, but he has no unique personality of his own. Robinson finally ends in this book by speaking of God as transpersonal and interpersonal rather than personal.[13]

Robinson calls his theology a "humanism within mystery." In his judgment this is a Christian humanism because it centers about the fulfillment of man. Our concern today, he maintains, is no longer how to find a gracious God, which occupied the attention of the Protestant Reformers. Rather it is how we can find a gracious neighbor. It is genuine community in the world that is the crying need today. Robinson insists that his humanism is Christian in that man's fulfillment has its basis in the prior gift of God's grace.

Robinson upholds love as the ultimate criterion for the moral life, but can love be separated from an encounter with the God who revealed himself in Jesus Christ? He says that if we give ourselves to love we shall find God, for God is love. Yet the New Testament would seem to indicate that *agape* is present only where faith in the living Christ is present (cf. John 14:23; 1 John 4:15, 16; 2 Cor. 5:14). Is not the love of God received only in faith? Robinson points to the fact that human love is universal, but is human love identical with *agape*?

This brings me to affirm that true love cannot be separated from the moral law. Jesus said that he had come not to abolish the law but to fulfill it. Yet the love of which both Robinson and Tillich speak would seem to transcend the law if not contradict it. When Robinson suggests that love might permit premarital sexual relations, does he not sever love from the law? When Tillich argues in the book *Ultimate Concern* that the time has come to dispense with life-long marriage vows and makes love the only standard and tie that unites a married couple, does not he dangerously verge towards antinomianism? Our ultimate criterion cannot simply be love, but rather it must be the revealed Word of God which unites love and truth.

Robinson, despite his admitted affinities with Tillich and Berdyaev, has difficulty in holding onto the mystical dimension of faith. There is little if any place in his theology for mystical prayer as this has been traditionally understood. For him prayer is basically reflection upon the needs of others and then rising to meet these needs. He sharply criticizes the mystical "flight of the alone to the alone," and there is some justification for this criticism. Robinson reminds us that Christ is to be found in the center of life and the midst of life. Yet does not our Lord also make himself present in the stillness of mystical meditation and interior prayer? For Robinson faith is an experience of that which is generally known in the world, namely, the power of love, not of that which is essentially beyond the world and the senses. In his theology faith is loyalty to the reality of love rather than mystical union with a Savior who died for our sins. He speaks much more kindly of mysticism in his *Exploration into God,* but what he affirms is a type of secularized or inverted mysticism by which we begin with politics and end in reflection upon the mystery of the world.[14] His latest writing seems to indicate that he is moving toward a synthesis of mysticism and secular theology, but what he proposes is a far cry from the Savior mysticism of the Bible.

Robinson upholds religionless Christianity and thereby would divorce faith from religion. By religion he means inwardness, metaphysics, and supernaturalism. He criticizes, for example, the metaphysical definitions of the incarnation, although he does not eschew metaphysics altogether. He contends that the resurrection of Christ must be understood not as a supernatural miracle but rather as a very natural awakening of the disciples to the significance of the cross. We must ask, though, whether the Christian faith can be severed from a supernaturalistic perspective. Should we not follow Karl Heim at this point and seek to reinterpret the supernatural rather than abandon this concept altogether? By seeking to divorce faith from its religious and metaphysical roots, Robinson ends in a Nestorian doctrine of Christ, a demythologized Gospel, a desupernaturalized eschatology and a despiritualized understanding of prayer.

In reaction against the separation of the sacred and secular Robinson nearly identifies them. In biblical religion the sacred is never confused with the secular but also never separated from it (cf. Lev. 10:10; Ps. 26:8; Ezek. 44:23). To distinguish the two is to place our relation to God on a different level from our relation to our fellowman, but by confusing the two Robinson loses the very essence of prayer and reinterprets it to mean serving our fellowman in love. He also loses sight of the real meaning of Holy Communion when he regards it as being on the same order as any common meal where faith and love are present. His belief that sex is a sacred act also manifests his inability to understand the distinction between the sacred and the secular. In the Bible the secular is potentially holy, but only because it can become a means or instrument of the sacred. Only God is holy in and of himself. Philip Micklem points out in his very provocative book *The Secular and the Sacred* that only in Hinduism are the sacred and the secular identified. In evangelical theology the secular can be turned toward the sacred but never transmuted into it. The secular can be at the most a sign and instrument of the holy.

Robinson's theology must be understood as a new kind of apologetics, one that is addressed to post-religious secular man. The basis for his apologetics lies in the universal experience of the depths of existence. The influence of Tillich can be seen at this point, but unlike Tillich, Robinson finds God in the midst of life rather than at the boundary of life.

The key to his apologetics lies in his inductive empirical approach to religion. Our starting point, he says, should be with Jesus as an ordinary human being. He affirms Jesus as the revelation of God because he is "the one who co-ordinates and vindicates for me all that I believe most deeply true." [15] If the love of God as revealed in Jesus meets and satisfies our deepest needs, if it brings meaning and joy to our life, then we can affirm the credibility and authority of the biblical witness. His criterion is pragmatic and empirical rather than dogmatic and authoritarian.

Robinson has said that his aim is to make God real for modern man. But does not Scripture tell us that only God can make himself real for men, and that he has done this in the life and death of Jesus Christ? Should not our task as ministers of the Gospel be to call men to acknowledge the distorted reality of their lives and to open themselves to the new reality that is Jesus Christ?

Robinson seems to speak not to convinced atheists but to modern doubters. He writes that his book *Honest to God* "has been welcomed not by the atheists nor by the religious but by those who say that it has given God back to them and made him real in a post-religious age." [16] But is he really reaching these people for

Christ or only for a non-personal or transpersonal God within the depths of existence, one which is in fact an idol? Robinson does point to Jesus as the final revelation of ultimate reality. But is Jesus only a prophetic figure who reveals divine love or is he the very God himself who has entered human flesh and taken upon himself the sins of a fallen race in his vicarious dying on the cross? Robinson's theology is still evolving, but thus far it seems that its focal point is not the God-Man who bore the sins of the world but only a universal law of love.

X.
Harvey Cox

Harvey Cox, an American Baptist theologian and professor of theology at Harvard University, is among those who are identified with the movement known as radical or secular theology. Like many of the other radical theologians, Cox recognizes that much of our traditional language concerning God is outmoded, but he believes that we can still speak of God as the moving force within and behind secular political events. Like Robinson he seeks to dereligionize the message of faith so that it can be more easily understood and accepted by modern man.

Cox terms his theology a "theology of social change." It is to be distinguished from both a theology of the Word of God as represented by Barth and a theology of religious experience which we find in Schleiermacher. The locus of revelation, according to Cox, is neither Holy Scripture nor the tradition of the church; rather it is to be equated with events of social change. The world-in-revolution is the theater of God's action. God is speaking to us not primarily in the creeds and symbols of the church but in the secular world. Revolutionary political movements today manifest the presence of God even more than the institutional church. Cox believes that such movements are inspired and directed by the Spirit of God; some secular theologians now call these movements "latent churches."

The criterion for truth in Cox's theology is pragmatic rather than metaphysical; the test of the validity of the Christian witness is whether it moves us to meet human need in the world today. The arena of salvation is the present struggle for social justice. Cox believes that the most important front in the social revolution today is racial integration. Salvation consists in creative freedom and humanization. He says little about the cross and resurrection of Jesus Christ; what is most important about Jesus is his life of exemplary love, his concern for the needy and the downtrodden, and his vicarious death on their behalf. Sin is defined as resistance to social change, as inertia and sloth. The need today is not for mystics who withdraw from the world but for Christian revolutionaries who seek to remake the world. The church is challenged by Cox to call its people to heroic suffering on behalf of the homeless and the outcasts in the modern world.

The doctrine of the kingdom of God plays an important role in Cox's theology. He holds with Barth that the kingdom has already been realized in the climactic life and death of Jesus Christ. He contends: "We are not fighting against a world with which we are at enmity; rather, it is a world in which a victory has already been achieved." [1] The demonic powers have been dethroned, although Cox insists that they continue to wage war. The church is one of the signs of the presence of the kingdom. The marks of the true church can no longer be regarded as the Word and sacraments, he maintains; rather they should be viewed as *koinonia, diakonia,* and *kerygma.* In other words, the church is known by its functions. Cox contends that revolutionary social movements are also signs of the kingdom. Even the secular city is a sign and witness of the kingdom of God. Here Cox's thinking appears similar to that of Gibson Winter, who in his book *New Creation As Metropolis* equates the emerging metropolitan complex with the "new creation." [2] Both Cox and Winter maintain that the secular city, the technopolis of the modern world, foreshadows and mirrors the *eschaton,* the new Jerusalem foretold in Scripture. This new metropolis, to be sure, is an ideal type which has not yet been perfectly realized, but the secular city as we know it signalizes the advent of the city of God.

Cox sees himself as standing in the line of the Social Gospel movement in American history. The "New Breed" of theologian which he upholds is renewing the quest for the kingdom of God on earth.[3] In his opinion the New Breed has a deeper understanding of the intransigence of evil than did the old Social Gospel theology. But in contradistinction to neo-orthodoxy, which views the kingdom as "an impossible possibility," the new Social Gospel sees it as something for which we ought to work. The theologians who comprise the New Breed are more appreciative of secular allies than were their spiritual forebears. They also envisage the church not so much as a vanguard but as a support for present secular movements of social reform.

Cox's theology is oriented about the secularization of modern life. He welcomes secularization, for to him it signifies the liberation of man from religious and metaphysical tutelage. It represents the turning of man's attention away from other worlds to this one. Secularization entails the relativization of all human values; the Christian can look favorably upon this development because of the biblical opposition to idolatry. Yet Cox acknowledges that secularization is also fraught with dangers; it can open the doorway to secularism, the absolutizing of the values of this world.

Cox follows Bonhoeffer in describing the modern secular man as the "man come of age." This kind of man stands in need of a secular Gospel which calls for the despiritualizing of our religious heritage. It beckons us to enter into the events and struggles of this world. A church that can speak to the modern age must be a church open to the world; the Christian must therefore devote himself not to speculation concerning a supernatural or heavenly realm but to the service of his brethren in this world. Cox sees the need for "creative disaffiliation" by which he means disengagement from trivial and perhaps also churchly tasks in order to gain the freedom to take part in the social and political struggles of our time. Creative disaffiliation represents the modern or secular form of asceticism. The sacraments are to be understood not as supernatural means of grace but as pledges of our dedication to social justice. Evangelism means not abstract preaching but social action, participation in the movement for social righteousness. The language of the Gospel must be neither mythical nor metaphysical but rather political, for politics is the only language that secular man readily understands.

Cox, like Robinson and Tillich, holds to situational ethics rather than an ethics of law. Not absolute principles but love must be the only criterion. Like Robinson he maintains that premarital and even extramarital sexual relations are justified in some circumstances. Cox holds that we should not seek to enforce upon our young people a code of conduct which is no longer relevant and which distorts the Gospel concerning Christian freedom. For him the basis of morality is not divine revelation but human need. In the past he has been very adamant in his opposition to the cult of sex as this is manifested in bathing beauty contests and girlie magazines. Sex must be accepted as a blessing of God's creation, but it must not be enthroned, he warns, for this is idolatry. Recently he has become more tolerant of such magazines as *Playboy*, and also more relativistic in his sexual ethics.

* * * * *

The theology of Harvey Cox can be welcomed as a breath of fresh air on the modern theological scene. Here is a man who is not afraid of urbanization and secularization. Here is a man who sees new opportunities for Christian witness in the secular urban world in which we find ourselves. Here is someone who faces the future with optimism, who even sees in the secular city a manifestation of the working of God.

Yet Cox's theology is certainly open to criticism. Any awareness of the tragic dimension of life appears to be missing, particularly in his description of the secular city. He does not fully take into account the oppression, crime, and utter loneliness which characterize the technopolis of today. He mentions these things, but his emphasis is on the advantages of urban life, such as anonymity and mobility. He also does not consider the fact that it is our cities which are marked for destruction in a world preparing for nuclear war. The brothers of Taizé have more accurately termed the secular city a "modern desert," the place where the demons abide and where they must be fought and overcome.

One can appreciate Cox's understanding of sin as slothfulness. Classical theology has always seen the two basic manifestations of sin as pride and sensuality or sloth, and it is this second aspect that has been neglected in modern theological circles. Medieval theologians regarded sloth as one of the seven deadly sins, and who can deny that this sin is particularly prevalent in America today? One must bear in mind that Cox is thinking not so much of idleness as of abdication of responsibility in the political realm, of apathy in the face of social injustice. Behind sloth, though, lies the rebellion of a fearful and unbelieving heart. Does Cox do justice to this other and deeper aspect of sin—the rebellion and perversion of the will, the hardness of heart which is the very core of sin? It would seem that Luther and Calvin and also Reinhold Niebuhr are much more profound in their treatment of the sinfulness of man.

Salvation is understood in Cox's theology in psychological and sociological terms, but he does not adequately relate soteriology to Christology. He speaks of reconciliation as the breaking down of the walls between men, but must not this reconciliation be grounded in another—the reconciliation of man with God in the sacrificial atoning death of Jesus Christ? We must recognize that justification as the Bible understands it has a much deeper meaning than the forgiving and accepting love which we experience in human relationships. Sanctification is not to be equated with either humanization or social integration.

Cox appears to empty the sacraments of all transcendent meaning. They become in his theology symbols of human commitment, pledges of loyalty to the cause of social righteousness. They are not regarded as supernatural means of grace. A sacrament is defined by Cox as "suffering with God in the world." [4] What is most crucial in the sacrament is no longer the action of God in Jesus Christ and the working of his Spirit but rather the depth of man's commitment to his brethren. It can be seen that in Cox's theology infant baptism has no meaning or value, since an infant cannot make a meaningful commitment to service in the world.

Cox maintains that the kingdom of God has already been realized in the advent of Jesus Christ. "It [the kingdom] has already been established, the victory has been won, and we are simply privileged to participate in the fruits of the new regime." [5] Our political message "does not urge or exhort people. It simply makes known what has happened, that 'the acceptable year of the Lord' has arrived." [6] But was not the kingdom merely announced and inaugurated by Jesus? The kingdom does not yet extend throughout the whole world. Niebuhr's understanding of the kingdom is in our estimation more realistic and more biblical. The kingdom is always coming, he writes, but it is never here. It will not be consummated or finalized until the end of world history. Niebuhr's biblical realism contrasts with the visionary but earnest idealism of Harvey Cox. In his latest writing Cox manifests a greater awareness of the difference between "the already" and "the not yet" in that he is now much more prone to refer to the kingdom as a task and goal as well as a present reality.

Cox calls the modern Christian to heroism or sainthood. He acknowledges that the kind of sainthood he supports is somewhat different from that upheld in the mystical and ascetical tradition of the church. He describes the new style saint as a revolutionary activist; he says that following Jesus today will make us participants in the social revolution. What he is seeking is the synthesis of two concepts—that of the saint and that of the revolutionary. But can the two be brought together? The saint has always been regarded in theological history as a man of prayer, humility, and godliness. In secular thought the hero has been noted as a man of superhuman courage and often boundless ambition. Nietzsche maintained that when God is dead we have come to the age of the superman. Though Cox's hero is not the same as the superman described by Nietzsche, he does bear a marked resemblance to the pioneering hero upheld by the Social Gospel movement in the early twenties.

There is admittedly a need today to cross dangerous frontiers, to break through into new patterns of Christian action, but is there not just as much need to draw close to the mystical wellsprings of the faith in prayer and meditation? Before we can participate effectively in the struggle for social and racial equality do we not need to be reborn as new creatures in faith and repentance? Is not the real arena of salvation the daily crisis of self-despair and repentance, and should not social action be the fruit and manifestation of this deeper inward struggle?

Cox has more recently sounded the call to a theology of celebration, which he seeks to hold in tension with a theology of social change. He now speaks of the secular quest for religious experience. Still, the worship experience that he has in mind is a far cry from the evangelical experience of repentance for sin.

It cannot be denied that Cox's theology is in large part apologetic, although he seeks to speak to the theological world as well as the world outside the church. One of his reasons for writing *The Secular City* was "to get those who inhabit the secular world to understand it and themselves in a historical-theological perspective." [7] He has sought to show how the Christian faith can be meaningful to the secular man of today, whether he be in or out of the church. In the process of arriving at a theological perspective that is culturally relevant he acknowledges that he has been led "to discount any supernatural 'overhead' or 'God-out-there.'" [8] With Leslie Dewart, whom he praises highly, he seeks a viable doctrine of God for our time, one that is "the most attractive alternative for the modern intelligence." [9]

Cox would have us believe that he stands closer to Barth and Bonhoeffer than to Tillich, and in some respects this is true, but at the same time it would seem that his underlying methodology is closer to that of Tillich.[10] Like Tillich and unlike Barth and Bonhoeffer he attempts to demonstrate the secular relevance of the Gospel. He seeks to correlate the biblical witness and contemporary cultural and political phenomena. In a similar manner to Tillich he speaks of an "answering theology" seeking to meet "the most salient features of the erupting new epoch." [11] In order to reach secular man for the Gospel he appeals to a common frame of reference: the world of politics. He has written:

> If neither "premetaphysical" nor existentialist language will reach urban-secular man, why do we believe a political theology will? The reason is that in secular society politics does what metaphysics once did. It brings unity and meaning to human life and thought.[12]

It is not Holy Scripture but the secular revolution which forms the subject matter of Cox's theology. He contends that the criterion for meaning is not given to man by God, but that it is man himself who "originates" meaning as he seeks to find himself in the world. Cox's theological starting point is not Jesus Christ the God-Man but Jesus the angry reformer.[13] He writes that theology should focus on the political scene, where man becomes man.[14] He endorses Ebeling's statement that "worldly talk of God is godly talk of the world." [15] He believes that the Christian and the natural man encounter the same reality, though they give it another name. This has been a basic principle of apologetic theology through the ages. Moreover, his admitted goal is to move secular man to enroll in the army of the kingdom of God. Although he speaks of the biblical proclamation as the means for attaining this goal, he has in mind not the preaching of the substitutionary atonement for sin but the heralding of the city of man and the call to freedom and responsibility in the new age in which we find ourselves. Our witness should consist, he says, in speaking about man, his needs and problems, and then acting to meet these needs. This is not apologetics in the old sense of defending God and religion, but it is a kind of secular validation of the faith.

Cox, like Bonhoeffer, speaks to the "world come of age" and the advent of secularization. Unlike Bonhoeffer, he does not regard the city of man or "the responsible society" as only a penultimate possibility. Instead, he identifies this earthly city with the eschatological kingdom of God. What Cox does not sufficiently discern is that it is not only religion that is in crisis today but the secular city itself. The secular and relativistic mood that dominates our culture is itself slowly but surely giving way to an era of barbarism and demonism. The demon of religion has been exorcized, but seven more demons are waiting to take its place (cf. Luke 11:24-26). Relativism is fostering a spirit of nihilism which is none other than the enthronement of chaos. Nihilism is another form of diabolism in which men sell their souls to the powers of evil. Are we not witnessing today the crumbling of the foundations of a predominantly secular culture and the recrudescence of the titanic gods of race, nation, and class? Perhaps what is needed in the dark age before us is the call to *diastasis* (separation) rather than to identification and solidarity with the world.

In reading Cox one cannot help wondering whether he has succumbed to the 19th century ideology of progress. He makes clear that his hope is for the realization of "the blessed community" on earth. In a manner reminiscent of Comte he views history in terms of three stages beginning with tribal culture, then proceeding to town culture and culminating in urban culture. In his *On Not Leaving It to the Snake* he traces the history of man's pilgrimage in terms of a movement from magical space to sacral space to secular space and finally to human space.[16] Christianity has been mainly responsible for moving Western culture "from the magical through the sacral stages of understanding space and place." Now we are at the beginnings of human space in which space is experienced "neither as malevolent nor as infinitely malleable." In this stage "places are understood as giving pace, variety, and orientation to man." The desacralization of space is the precondition for its humanization. He believes, however, that the new age of humanization will not come to us automatically and that much agony and struggle lie before us. At times he appears to recognize that the new world city augurs not only hope but also despair, but his emphasis is undoubtedly on the former. Yet as Tillich and others have reminded us, although the modern world has experienced technical and material progress, it surely does not know of any moral and spiritual progress. Indeed, if the things of the spirit are the criteria for progress, then we can only conclude that man has descended to a new infancy.

Cox and other secular theologians are on firm ground when they maintain that the language of the pulpit is meaningless today for most people. It is not an exaggeration to speak of a famine of the Word of God. Yet can it be that people are not hearing God's Word because God is withholding himself, because God refuses to send forth his Spirit? And is not God withholding himself because of the doublemindedness and hypocrisy of his representatives, because of the widespread apostasy of his children? That this idea is solidly scriptural cannot be gainsaid (cf. Isa. 63:15; Jer. 12:7, 8; Hos. 5:6; Amos 8:11, 12). Is not the crying need today heartfelt repentance for national and personal sins rather than a new kind of terminology or a new type of missionary strategy? Is not Bonhoeffer more correct than some of his latter-day disciples when he intimates that we need to wait and pray for the Spirit of God before we can again preach with power and authority?[17] He rightly insists that God must act in his own time before we can speak in a new Spirit-filled language. Is not the key to Christian renewal in our day a new outpouring of the Holy Spirit?

XI.
Thomas Altizer

One cannot write on the subject of the Christian witness in a secular age without giving serious attention to the death-of-God theology represented by such thinkers as Altizer, Wm. Hamilton, Rubenstein, van Buren, and Harrison. This movement can be described as the radical wing of the new secular theology.

Thomas Altizer is an Episcopal layman and professor of English at the State University of New York at Stony Brook. Previously he was a teacher of religion at Emory University, Atlanta, Georgia. Both Hamilton and van Buren are ordained clergymen in the American Baptist and Episcopal churches respectively, and both have taught theology in theological seminaries, although they are now teaching at secular institutions.

Like many secular theologians (such as Cox and Robinson) the death-of-God votaries uphold a form of religionless Christianity. They go further, however, in asserting that the concept of God, indeed the very reality of God, is questionable, and that faith needs to be centered about human values and experiences. Such thinkers as Altizer and Rubenstein still make a place for mysticism, but it is a mysticism of this world, a profane or secularized mysticism characterized not by the negation of the world but by immersion in the creative powers and energies of the world.

The death-of-God theology cannot properly be understood apart from the penetration of secularism into the modern world and church. The hallmark of modern culture is a loss of faith in the transcendent, and the death-of-God theologians address themselves to this situation. They are attempting to break through the indifference of the modern world to the meaning of faith. They seek a faith that is both relevant and contemporary, one that speaks to the modern mind. As Altizer has expressed it: "If there is one clear portal to the twentieth century, it is a passage through the death of God, the collapse of any meaning or reality beyond the newly discovered radical immanence of modern man, an immanence dissolving even the memory or the shadow of transcendence." [1]

The death-of-God theologians, particularly Altizer, van Buren, and Hamilton, typify a marked reaction against neo-orthodoxy, the new religious establishment. Whereas the neo-orthodox theologians have upheld God as a personal being, the new radical theology contends that this God is dead, that he has disappeared from the modern historical consciousness. For Altizer and Hamilton God's death is a historical event of great magnitude and significance for modern man. Neo-orthodox theology sought to recall the church to the authority of the Bible, but the death-of-God theologians substitute the authority of human experience. In neo-orthodoxy Jesus is upheld as the Savior from sin, the Mediator; in the new radical theology Jesus is the pattern, the model, the "man for others." Altizer sometimes describes him as an unfolding creative process in the world. For the neo-orthodox theologians the theme of theology can be none other than the message of the cross, the Gospel of reconciliation and redemption. For both Altizer and Hamilton the death of God is the theme of theology, although the latter also gives much attention to a secular style of life. Theologians such as Barth and Brunner are noted for their emphasis on the uniqueness of the atonement or the Christ event. According to Altizer the atonement is a universal process, "a process present wherever there is life and energy, wherever alienation and repression are abolished by the self-negation of their ultimate source." [2] Finally, dialectical theology has been primarily pessimistic as far as human capabilities are concerned, but radical theology is optimistic.[3] As Hamilton reminds us, though, this is not the optimism of grace but a worldly optimism, one that is based on man's own power and reason. Altizer contends that we are now entering the Age of the Spirit, the age that marks the fulfillment of the creative world process. To be sure, he also speaks of a present darkness and of a new epiphany of the Antichrist, but he identifies this with the "final kenotic manifestation of Christ." [4] According to Hamilton, Christian theology no longer needs to consider the tragic element in life, because tragedy requires the presence of God or gods.[5]

Despite these disagreements, though, there are certain basic similarities between the new radical theology and neo-orthodoxy. First, the new radicals concur with the Barthians that Christianity signifies the negation of religion. They also share the neo-orthodox distrust of proofs and evidences for faith. Both Altizer and Hamilton stress the need to walk solely by faith, even though they cannot maintain this posture because of their appeal to the modern consciousness. Like Barth, Brunner, and Niebuhr the radicals contend that Christianity means freedom from the law, although they extend this to include freedom from biblical and ecclesiastical traditions as well.

In order to understand the significance of the new radicals, we must ask what they mean by the term "the death of God." Since this chapter concerns Altizer in particular, we shall concentrate on his views, but we cannot understand this theologian apart from the wider movement in which he stands. Gabriel Vahanian, who does not really belong to the school of radical theology, has in mind a cultural death of God. Van Buren contends that any reference to God is nonsense in the modern empirical age; his position might be denominated an extreme agnosticism.[6] Altizer and Hamilton speak of a historical death of God, meaning that God has actually died in human history. For Hamilton this means the experience of the absence of God and not the absence of the experience of God. In his earlier writings he described the modern period as one of waiting for God, but he has now abandoned this terminology. For Altizer the death of God is a historical event which he equates with the death of Christ on the cross. The impact of God's death was not fully realized, however, until the nineteenth century, and this is why we may speak of God's death as occurring in the modern age.

Let us examine Altizer's views in greater depth. When Altizer speaks of the death of God, he is referring to the God of Christendom, the God of biblical religion. As we shall see, he has not grasped the full meaning of the God of the Bible, since the God that he refers to is not wholly transcendent. He leans heavily on both Nietzsche and William Blake in his understanding of the death of God. It was Nietzsche who first used this term in the modern age and who gave it philosophical significance. Altizer accepts Nietzsche's idea of "Eternal Recurrence," the perpetual reappearance of Being in new form. In Altizer's words, "Only when God is dead can Being begin in every now." [7] William Blake identified God with Jesus and therefore also in a sense affirmed the death of God. He equated the God of historical Christianity with Satan who died so that the spirit of Jesus could live on in the hearts of men. Altizer accepts the vision of Blake and seeks to build upon it.[8]

Another philosopher who has been of immense aid to Altizer is Hegel. Hegel envisaged God as Absolute Mind which negated itself and entered into human history. He saw the consummation of history as the return of the Absolute Spirit into itself in an enduring synthesis of the material and the spiritual. Altizer accepts this dialectic movement of God from thesis to antithesis to a final synthesis when the world will realize its identity with God. Like Hegel, Altizer holds that God entered the world decisively in Jesus Christ and ceased therefore to be static, transcendent, and absolute. What Altizer has in mind is a transformation of God rather than the literal death of God as a person. He describes this in terms of the incarnation of the divine spirit, but what he means is a metamorphosis rather than a genuine incarnation. God does not simply assume human flesh; he becomes flesh, the world, history. The sacred enters into the profane and transmutes the profane into itself. Altizer contends that this is a liberating message because it means that God is now in man realizing himself in human creativity and productivity. It also means that man need no longer be enslaved to the God of Christian tradition who terrorizes and condemns. This is why he speaks of his vision as a "gospel," the "gospel of Christian atheism."

His point of view might be described as an evolutionary process philosophy in that he sees the world-Spirit, whom he calls "Christ," realizing itself progressively in world history. Here one can discern his affinities with Chardin and Whitehead. Altizer also has definite links with Platonic philosophy, although there are some notable differences as well. Like Plato and the Platonic tradition generally Altizer sees the fall in terms of the transition from essence to existence. But unlike Plato Altizer understands the salvation of man in terms of the transformation or sacralization of existence. With Tillich, whom he hails as the father of modern radical theology, he affirms the death of the God of theism. But he believes the answer lies not in the affirmation of a God beyond God but in the realization that man is God, that human consciousness is the locus of divinity.

Altizer's theology might aptly be called a new form of mysticism, but it is the profane mysticism of Nietzsche rather than classical Christian mysticism which he espouses. Contact with the divine is not simply in the inner spirit of man but in the passage of human experience. As he remarks: "The Center is everywhere, eternity begins in every Now." [9] Altizer has been deeply influenced by Eastern mysticism. Indeed, he was a student of Joachim Wach, professor of the history of religions at the University of Chicago, and was tremendously influenced by Wach's successor Mircea Eliade. He wrote his doctoral thesis at Chicago in the field of the history of religions with special emphasis upon Eastern mysticism.[10] Like the mystics of the East Altizer affirms an original primal unity, but unlike these mystics he seeks not a return to this unity but a breakthrough into a new kind of unity. His is an eschatological mysticism in which the *coincidentia oppositorum*, the joining of the opposites of sacred and profane, is realized in a new synthesis. Like both Eastern and Christian mystics he envisages prayer as an opening of oneself to the divine center rather than as supplication. With Meister Eckhart he views Jesus as the historical sign of the birth of the Son of God in the human soul.

Altizer's position can be legitimately described as atheistic, since he views the cross as the self-annihilation of God. Yet since in his theology God reappears in a new form as the incarnate evolving Christ, his is not a consistent atheism. His philosophy is perhaps more accurately described as pantheistic. Indeed, he has called it "a dynamic-process pantheism." [11] It can also be termed monistic, since he views reality as being essentially all of one piece. For Altizer there is no God, nor has there ever been a God who created the world out of nothing and who stands above the processes of nature. For him God was originally a part of the primal totality out of which both deity and world evolved.

* * * * *

In giving an appraisal of Altizer's theology we should first compare him with the other secular and radical theologians. First, it should be seen that there is a definite similarity between his position and that of such thinkers as Cox, Hamilton, and Robinson. All of these men are essentially optimistic in outlook. They follow Bonhoeffer in speaking of the world come of age and of man coming to adulthood. Just as Cox regards the secular city as the prime manifestation of the dawning kingdom of God, so Altizer (like his mentor William Blake) sees America as the place where the apocalyptic freedom of the Christian will be realized. Altizer follows Joachim of Floris in speaking of the new Age of the Spirit, and he contends that we are now entering this messianic age. Like the other radical theologians, Altizer seeks a contemporary faith, one that will be meaningful to the post-modern secularized man. In contrast to such thinkers as Cox and Hamilton, Altizer's orientation is more inner-worldly than this-worldly. He begins not with the world as such but with a vision of the world. His concern is not a secular style of life so much as it is immersion in the depths of existence. His interest is more metaphysical than ethical; he is not a church reformer like Cox and Robinson but rather a religious revolutionary, one who seeks to transform the message of faith itself.

Altizer speaks much of Christ, and like Hamilton his orientation is markedly Christological. Kenosis is the key concept in his Christology: God emptying himself and incarnating himself in the person of Jesus and in all humanity. For Altizer God is transmuted into flesh, into man, so that it is possible to hold that God is Jesus but not that Jesus is God. What he is talking about, as we have said, is a metamorphosis rather than an authentic incarnation in which God retains his essential nature. Jesus Christ is not a divine person who assumes human flesh but rather the human vessel which embodies the discarnate God. Altizer resurrects the heresy of Patripassianism when he asserts that God the Father suffers on the cross and not simply the man Jesus. Moreover, instead of a resurrection from the dead, Altizer affirms a continuing incarnation in which the Absolute Spirit incarnates itself more fully into the human race. The descent into hell does not mean a descent into the nether world of spirits but rather the descent of the Christ Spirit ever more fully into darkness and flesh. The death of God continues, therefore, and it will not be fully realized until the discarnate God is all in all. But this is a parody of the Gospel message that God in Christ conquered death. Altizer has a doctrine of the cross but not of the resurrection. Yet Paul rightly saw that if Christ be not raised, then our faith is in vain (1 Cor. 15:17).

For Altizer, salvation consists not in divine forgiveness but in enlightenment, in the knowledge of God's death. Kenneth Hamilton is correct when he labels this a form of Gnosticism, since it substitutes esoteric knowledge for faith in the living God.[12] Altizer speaks of faith, but he means not trust in a divine Person but the apprehension of a divine process in the world. His theology signalizes the wedding of Christianity and esoteric mysticism.

Altizer stands in the tradition of radical Christianity in that his orientation is incontestably eschatological. He looks forward to the coming apocalyptic, the final union between the immanent world Spirit and humanity. Like many of the radical Christians in ages past he envisages a cosmic reversal, an Antichrist, and a new creation. He speaks even of the regeneration of the entire universe. Yet it should be noted that this final consummation signifies the fulfillment of immanent forces and not supernatural divine intervention.

Unlike many of the secular theologians, Altizer seeks to take hell, guilt, and despair seriously. He berates modern theology for being mute on the subject of damnation. "Why can the theologian not speak of Hell, whereas the artist and the thinker often seem to speak of nothing else?" [13] Yet for Altizer hell is the arena of human existence; it is existence with guilt. Its terror is rooted in ignorance rather than in the judgment and wrath of God against sin. Altizer views the source of guilt as the "clinging to the wholly alien power of a now emptied transcendent realm." [14] Freedom from guilt lies in the denial of the existence of God. "If we can truly know that God is dead, and can fully actualize the death of God in our own experience, then we can be liberated from the threat of condemnation, and freed from every terror of a transcendent beyond." [15] This is a far cry from the biblical view that freedom from guilt lies in a recognition of divine forgiveness and in personal repentance from sin.

Altizer, Hamilton, van Buren, and some of the other radicals all seek to move beyond apologetics in that they are no longer interested in defending the claims of Christian faith before the bar of reason. Yet the apologetic concern persists in these men. We read in their writings of the need to be "authentically contemporary" and to make the symbols of faith "meaningful to the modern consciousness." [16] Altizer holds that "we must confess that God has died if this is the path to the fully profane moment of our time." [17] His view is that faith "must now find a trans-Christian language . . . if it is to exist and to live as faith." [18] This is not a defense of Christianity so much as it is an attempt to preserve a framework of meaning that will give direction to modern man in his quest. At times Altizer can sound almost "evangelistic" in his desire to convince modern man of the contemporaneity of the new gospel of Christian atheism. He calls upon the reader "to open himself to Christ who is fully present, the Christ who has completed a movement from transcendence to immanence, and who is kenotically present in . . . the immediacy of the actual moment before us." [19]

Here we can discern the final end of the old liberal apologetic theology. In an attempt to make the faith palatable to the cultured despisers of religion, the theologians have ended in capitulating to the spirit of the age. Instead of building on a criterion held in common with the culture, the modernist theologian has finally been compelled to abandon the Christian criterion altogether and accept the presuppositions of secular philosophy. Unlike Cox and Robinson, the death-of-God theologians do not seek to translate the Gospel into the idiom of the modern age but rather to transform the Gospel itself so that it becomes practically identical with the spirit of the age.[20] Indeed, they do not seek for "relevance or contemporaneity for its own sake"; instead they "strive for a whole new way of theological understanding." [21] The result is a new gospel, which Altizer calls "the gospel of Christian atheism" and which Hamilton terms "the new essence of Christianity." What Altizer gives us is a new *gnosis,* but not the renewal of faith. The norm for both Altizer and Hamilton is no longer divine revelation but contemporary existence.

It has been said that when God is dead, then the gods are reborn. Both Altizer and Hamilton speak of a new radical epiphany for our age. Both of these men seem to locate the new domain of the sacred in the experience of sex. Hamilton has suggested that not only sex but nonmarital sex can be thought of as an emerging form of the sacred.[22] Altizer hails William Blake, who saw the world of generation as the body of Christ. It was Blake who held that "sexual generation" is "the most immediate arena of the process of regeneration." [23] For Blake the "passion of sex" is "the most immediate epiphany" of a redemptive energy.[24] Altizer also embraces Nietzsche's ideal of Dionysian existence which entails the "baptism of the instincts" and vitalistic intoxication.[25] Like Rubenstein, the Jewish death-of-God theologian, Altizer seems to uphold a return to the gods of nature; this is indeed a new mystical paganism.

Like most of the radical secular theologies the death-of-God theology lends support to the new morality; indeed, it can be said that it promotes moral anarchy. Altizer subscribes to the Nietzschian verdict that the emancipated man is "beyond good and evil." He affirms: "Good and evil cease to be when man is delivered from selfhood. . . ." [26] He would indubitably concur with Ivan Karamazov: "If there is no God, all things are permissible." At a symposium at Northwestern University in 1966 he argued that since divine authority had collapsed "there was absolutely no basis for moral decision-making." [27] Civil rights was labeled a phony issue by Altizer, and he refused to give any moral directives on the Vietnam situation. What Altizer upholds is a kind of ethical nihilism. Nevertheless, he is much more consistent than such thinkers as Cox and Robinson in that he recognizes that when there are no longer any moral absolutes, there can also not be any ethics.

William Braden hails Altizer as the prophet of the new age.[28] He contends that Altizer's philosophy speaks to the contemporary man who is asking ultimate questions and who seeks final answers. Altizer, unlike most of the secular theologians, is also open to the thought of the East, and in Braden's view pantheistic mysticism is the religion of the future. What Braden recognizes is that Altizer's syncretistic philosophy is peculiarly adapted to the mood of our times. But as Pascal saw, the God of Abraham, Isaac, and Jacob is not the God of the philosophers. This must be affirmed even when, as in Altizer's theology, this God is called the Spirit of Christ. Even Altizer himself acknowledges that the world-Spirit which he upholds is antithetical to the transcendent God of Scripture and church tradition.

Martin Buber is far more acute than the death-of-God theologians when he speaks of an eclipse of God rather than the death of God.[29] God is still present, but something has come between man and God which makes man oblivious to this divine presence. The problem of the modern age according to Buber is unbelief; what antagonizes modern man is not God so much as faith. What people today as in every age need is not a new world view but a divine Gospel, not a new *gnosis* but a living faith.

XII.
Beyond Apologetics: A Restatement of the Christian Witness

It can be said that what is wrong with the latest wave of apologetic and philosophical theology is that it knows "neither the scriptures nor the power of God" (Mark 12:24). The new theology is anchored in the spirit of the age and the values of the culture rather than in the biblical revelation. It is eclectic and syncretistic rather than catholic and evangelical. Its reliance is not on the Holy Spirit but on human power and reason. This is why we must seek an alternative to this kind of theology if we are to remain faithful to Christ in carrying out the great commission to preach the Gospel to the whole creation (Mark 16:15).

What is needed today is a bold and fresh restatement of the Christian message, one that is solidly anchored in Scripture. Our task is to confront a radically secular world with the Gospel of reconciliation and redemption. This message must be made intelligible to modern man, but at the same time it cannot be amalgamated with secular philosophy. We must witness to the Word of God, which stands over against all man-made culture and brings all human values and goals under divine judgment. This same Word calls the church to repentance and reformation.

First it is necessary to show why we must look beyond an apologetic theology if we are to render a relevant and compelling witness to Jesus Christ. Apologetics is here understood as the attempt to make the faith plausible to the world of unbelief on the basis of a criterion held in common with unbelief. Our questioning of the validity of apologetics in this sense is based partly on a study of the close relationship between apologetic theology and heresy in the history of the church, as well as on the role of apologetic theology in the progressive secularization of modern culture. Yet despite this historical confirmation our principal reasons for questioning the apologetic venture as this has been traditionally understood are solidly theological. We shall proceed to examine these theological arguments.

It must first be recognized that the natural man is incapable of making a positive decision on his own for the Gospel. Luther was right in saying that man's will is in bondage to forces and powers beyond his control. Psychoanalysis and Marxist philosophy have drawn our attention to some of these powers, but Christian theology alone perceives the deepest and most insidious power—original sin. Man is not merely afflicted by sin, but he has become a willing servant of sin. He is no longer able to receive the Spirit of truth because his senseless mind is darkened (John 14:17; Rom. 1:21). Paul contended that "the mind that is set on the flesh is hostile to God; it does not submit to God's law, indeed it *cannot*" (Rom. 8:7, italics mine). In Paul's theology the natural man is dead in sin (Col. 2:13; Eph. 2:1, 5); man must be raised from the death of sin by the quickening Spirit of God before he can commit his life to Christ. He must be empowered and directed by the Spirit if he is to find his way into the kingdom. Jesus made this very clear: "No one can come to me unless the Father who sent me draws him" (John 6:44). The natural man is involved not so much in the abuse of freedom, as Niebuhr maintains, but in slavery. The preacher of the Gospel must appeal therefore not to the wisdom or powers of man but to the Spirit of God who alone can unshackle the chains that bind us to the old order. He must seek not the favor of his hearers but the blessing of God (Gal. 1:10), since it is only the holy God who converts the hearts of sinners.

Secondly, the natural man does not seek the truth of the Gospel; consequently it is ludicrous to try to correlate this truth with the searchings and strivings of the culture. The biblical picture of man shows that he is in flight from God, not that he seeks God. Adam after his sin sought to hide from God (Gen. 3:8). Man does not come to the light because he fears that his evil deeds might be exposed (John 3:19, 20). Karl Barth accurately describes the natural state of man: "We are fundamentally fearful of the stream of God's righteousness which seeks entrance into our life and our world."[1] And in the words of John Calvin: "Human reason . . . neither approaches, nor tends, nor directs its view towards truth, to understand who is the true God, or in what character he will manifest himself to us."[2] To be sure, once man is confronted by the Holy Spirit he then is impelled to seek for God. But as Pascal said, putting words into the mouth of Christ, "You would not seek me if you had not found me."

Apologetic theologians, particularly modernists, are prone to speak of a universal quest for God, but the Bible knows nothing of such a quest. Man yearns and longs for God, but does he seek God? Man was set on earth in order to seek God (Acts 17:27), but in actual fact it is his own glory that he seeks (Phil. 2:21). Niebuhr maintains that man is fundamentally directed toward God but that his searchings and yearnings are negated as well as fulfilled by the Christian revelation. Tillich speaks of a correlation between the natural quest for meaning and security and the Gospel. In his view men of every race and religion seek and ask for the Christian answer. But do these views do justice to Paul's: ". . . no one understands, no one seeks for God" (Rom. 3:11, cf. Ps. 14:2, 3)? Do not they also go against these words of Scripture: "I was ready to be sought by those who did not ask for me; I was ready to be found by those who did not seek me" (Is. 65:1)? Job asked whether man by searching can find out God (11:7 KJV). Indeed, the truth of the matter is that we do not ever find God, but we are found by God when we meet the living Savior, Jesus Christ.

A third reason for calling the apologetic enterprise into question is that the truth of faith is not amenable to rational appropriation. Paul describes the Word of God as unsearchable and inscrutable (Rom. 11:33; cf. Is. 55:8, 9). Kierkegaard spoke of the "infinite qualitative difference" between God and man; by this he meant that God's truth is beyond the reach of man's conception and perception. Only faith can lay hold of God's Word, and it does so without human power or aid (Luther). Reason can be utilized in the service of faith, and then it becomes faithful reasoning, but even a reason illumined by faith can know God's Word only dimly and brokenly. God remains hidden even in the act of revelation. He speaks to us, never directly but always through the word of the sermon, the bread and wine of the sacrament, or a deed of loving mercy. Man can truly hear the Word of God, but he cannot fully comprehend the significance of what is disclosed to him. As the Psalmist said: "Such knowledge is too wonderful for me; it is high, I cannot attain it" (139:6). The Word of God is like a blinding light which cannot really be seen but which makes an indelible impression upon the soul. This Word or truth can be experienced but never fully appropriated; it must be sought again and again. Our knowledge of God is always in the form of remembrance *(anamnesis)*, never in the form of possession.

Again, Paul makes clear that the means chosen by God for the redemption of men is the foolishness of preaching (Rom. 10:17; 1 Cor. 1:21-25; 2 Cor. 5:19, 20; Gal. 3:2). He testifies that men cannot know God through worldly wisdom (1 Cor. 1:21). Paul had utilized an apologetic approach in Athens, but when he arrived in Corinth he said that he would preach only Christ and him crucified (1 Cor. 2:2). It is interesting to note that in Paul's address in Athens, it was only when he began to preach the resurrection that some were aroused to opposition and others to belief (Acts 17:32-34). One might consequently hold that an apology which appeals to the wisdom of the world can only be an instrument of saving grace insofar as it contains the glad tidings of redemption. Luther voiced the general Reformation position concerning the source of faith: "Thus there is no other means of attaining faith than by hearing, learning, and pondering the Gospel." [3] The New Testament makes clear that deeds of mercy and sacramental acts can also be a means of salvation, but only when related to and illumined by the preaching and hearing of the word of the cross. This is why both Calvin and Luther maintained that the sacrament depends upon the Word for its efficacy.

Moreover, it must be recognized that the Word of God is self-authenticating. The Word is not simply Scripture, but the whole self-revelation of God in Christ to which Scripture attests. It is the entire revelatory message of Scripture, the Gospel of salvation. This Word is the ground and center of all meaning; it cannot possibly be buttressed by the fragmentary meanings of human culture and philosophy. The Gospel of God contains its own principle of interpretation. It provides its own evidence: the assurance of forgiveness and the joy of salvation.

It is only in the light of the Word that we are able to perceive light (Ps. 36:9; John 1:9). The men on the way to Emmaus were persuaded by the very force of the words of Christ and the testimony of Scripture (Luke 24:32). The eunuch was convinced simply by Philip's explication of the meaning of Scripture (Acts 8:26-40). One can be convicted of his sin and awakened to the truth only by the Spirit or the power of the Word itself. One must hear Christ speaking to him personally in the depths of his soul, and only then can he really believe. As the converts said to the Samaritan woman: "'It is no longer because of your words that we believe, for we have heard for ourselves, and we know that this is indeed the Savior of the world'" (John 4:42).

* * * * *

In seeking to restate the Christian message we must recall to mind the ultimate criterion of our faith, that is, divine revelation. Revelation is the incursion of the sacred or the holy into the realm of the secular; it is to be understood as God's self-disclosure of his love and mercy to the believer. Where has revelation taken place? First of all, it has occurred in the sacred history attested to and mirrored in the Bible. The climax or fulfillment of this history is the life, death, and resurrection of Jesus Christ. Revelation therefore signifies the objective action of God in biblical history and particularly in the personal history of Jesus Christ.

Revelation, though, also takes place in religious experience. Revelation has not only an objective but also a subjective pole, the experience of faith. Consequently, revelation might be defined as the conjunction of divine-revealing action and human response. When we say that Jesus Christ is the norm we mean not only the Jesus of history but also the indwelling Christ, the mystical Christ.

Revelation involves not only personal encounter between God

and man but also the disclosure of meaning. Barth has said that revelation consists in word as well as deed. Or as Tillich has put it, the event of revelation is a syndrome of fact and interpretation. Revelation does not overthrow reason but establishes it on a new foundation. The truth of revelation is not suprarational or irrational, but rather rational in the proper sense. This truth can and must be received by reason. But this possibility lies on the side of revelation. Revelation cannot be assimilated by the processes of thought, but it can integrate and reorient thinking. It cannot be established or disputed scientifically, but it can give meaning to the totality of human experience once it is accepted.

Revelation is not exhausted when we describe it in terms of personal encounter, nor even when we include the element of spiritual wisdom. Its deepest meaning is reconciliation, salvation. Revelation brings us not only new knowledge but saving knowledge. It brings to us the "new being." It signifies a message which not only informs but transforms.

The message of revelation concerning the salvation of Jesus Christ should be the foundation of all Christian theology. The theme of theology is not the translation of this message to the culture, as Bultmann maintains, but the message of revelation itself. This message might be equated with the kerygma, but the kerygma has a determinative content. It consists of more than simply the assurance of forgiveness; it signifies Jesus Christ, his virgin birth, his life and death, his resurrection and ascension. The message of revelation is none other than the mystery of the plan of salvation. The dramatic acts of God form the core of this message, but these acts can be expressed only in mythical or imaginative picture language. We maintain against Bultmann that myth is the necessary vehicle of this message; although the apostolic witness must be reinterpreted it can finally be expressed only in the picture language of Canaan.

The task of theology is to correlate the language of the church not with the self-understanding of the culture but with the meaning of the Word. This means that in order to explicate the truths of revelation we must penetrate behind the mythical language even though we dare not abandon it. It also means that we must express the spiritual wisdom given in revelation in doctrinal form, for the message implies doctrine. Doctrine is not the reconciliation or synthesis of several diverse elements but rather an analytical development of the central fact of revelation. It is an implication of the fact, form, and content of revelation.

To proclaim the saving message, therefore, also means to preach doctrinally, even though we must remember that there are no revealed doctrines as such. The vicarious suffering of Christ on the cross implies the doctrine of the substitutionary atonement. The incarnation of the Word and the gift of the Spirit imply the doctrine of the Trinity. In other words, even in a secular age we must preach doctrine as well as a message. We preach doctrine to clarify and safeguard the message. The doctrine of predestination, for example, protects and illumines the message that God loved us while we were yet in our sins.

The heart of our proclamation, however, must not be doctrine but the "good news" concerning God's atoning, reconciling work in Jesus Christ. But we should remember that this atoning work is efficacious only for faith. The message of revelation is incontrovertibly theocentric, since it is concerned with God's glory. But it is at the same time radically anthropocentric because it is concerned with man's eternal salvation. Therefore this message implies not only theology in the narrow sense, i.e., the doctrine of God, but also anthropology, the discipline which treats of the nature and destiny of man. But against Bultmann and Robinson I hold that this is an anthropology rooted in Christology.

With Barth we contend that revelation must be proclaimed, not defended or even recommended in the sense of trying to heighten its value. It must be told, not taught (Brunner). To be sure, the truths of revelation can and must be taught, but the place for formal teaching or *didache* (which includes the exposing of false doctrine) is in the community of faith. This is not to deny that biblical preaching will include teaching just as Christian teaching will include preaching; yet the teaching aspect must be centered in the heralding of the glad news of redemption.[4]

Again I agree with Barth that revelation must be proclaimed in an intelligible manner. We must not simply preach outworn clichés, which are sometimes mistakenly identified with the "simple Gospel." Instead we must present a logically coherent message, one which is in the language of our hearers. We must take care to do away with all false stumbling-blocks that stand in the way of the acceptance of the Gospel, such as crass biblical literalism, so that men can be confronted with the authentic scandal of the cross.

It is even permissible to utilize secular categories and thought forms in order to communicate the Christian message. Yet in doing so we must be extremely cautious, since the danger is that the secular or ideological meanings associated with these terms might usurp the meaning of the cross. A term such as "humanization," for example, may or may not be equivalent to what the Bible understands by sanctification. It depends on the context in which this term is used and whether or not it has been properly baptized into the life and thought of the Christian church. Secular and philosophical terms and categories must be subordinated to biblical meanings or else the door will be open for a philosophical or natural theology in which the uniqueness of the Christian revelation will be subverted.

It is possible to baptize secular categories because men have been created in the image of God and thereby still reflect some of the wisdom and goodness of their Creator despite the fall. Also, the Spirit works even in the natural man, though against his will and in opposition to his general orientation toward life. It is in fact mandatory to baptize secular terms because sinful man has used such terms in the service of an idolatrous structure of meaning.

It must be recognized that communication entails more than simply making the message of faith intelligible. It means making the message knowable, and only the Holy Spirit does that. Communication consists therefore not merely in the imparting of information but in the transmission of meaning and power. As Paul wrote: "For our gospel came to you not only in word, but also in power and in the Holy Spirit and with full conviction" (1 Thess. 1:5). To communicate the Gospel, then, is to present it to our hearers in such a way that they can make an existential response. Our communication is not effectual unless it elicits not only serious consideration but surrender and dedication. Our hearers have not heard the Word of God unless they have been transformed from spectators into participants.

The danger in the method of correlation which Tillich and Niebuhr advocate is that it lets the life-situations of the hearers determine the content of our message. The temptation is to build on the questions of culture rather than on the answer of faith. The truth is that we cannot ask the right questions until we know the ultimate answer. The correlation that we should aim for is therefore one between the message of the church and revelation.

We also have serious questions about the apologetic method of attack, what Emil Brunner calls "eristics." This method entails the destruction of the intellectual framework of unbelief in order to drive our hearers into creative despair. Reinhold Niebuhr has popularized this method in this country. The danger in eristics is that the theme of the sermon becomes not the good news of redemption but the idolatry and ambiguity of the culture. There is a place for attacking modern towers of Babel, but we should let the Gospel pull these towers down. The Gospel does not need our help. Niebuhr seeks to break down culture idolatry by unmasking the antinomies and contradictions in secular philosophy. Such an approach can be meaningful within the circle of faith, but what the unbeliever needs to hear is the word of salvation. A word of judgment must accompany this saving word, but it should never be spoken apart from the message of salvation.

Bonhoeffer is right when he argues that prayer and meditation are the soil out of which a potent Gospel proclamation must come. He reminds us that prayer evangelism must precede the preaching of the Word. Indeed to be replenished with the Holy Spirit is the prerequisite for vital Gospel preaching. Can it be said that the devotional life is the lost dimension in modern Protestantism, and that before we can earnestly think of seeking and saving the lost we must recover the hidden discipline of devotion? Is there not a need to strengthen our bond with the sacred before we can minister in and to the secular?

The hidden discipline, however, must bear fruit in Gospel preaching. Such preaching means to share the story of Christ, to tell others of what God has done for the world and for us personally in the momentous acts of salvation climaxing in Calvary. We must relate the message to our hearers by entering their situation. The distinction between life-situation and expositional sermons is artificial, for every sermon must be both; it must begin from the Bible and proceed to the cultural situation. Barth has rightly said that the two things necessary for an intelligible witness are the Bible and the daily newspaper.

Again I contend that we must not only preach the good news but also warn our hearers of God's judgment. Barth maintains that when we speak to the man outside the church we should concentrate on the love of God revealed in Christ. Yet can we preach the Gospel without speaking about the law? The law must be proclaimed with the Gospel and in the context of the Gospel, but it must be preached. We must speak the truth in love, but this truth will burn because the fire of God's love also signifies his wrath against sin and injustice. In other words, true Christian preaching must be prophetic as well as kerygmatic. It will seek to bring the values and goals of the culture under the judgment of God. It will remind people that the day of the Lord is a day of darkness for those who persist in iniquity (cf. Amos 5:20; Joel 2:2).

Finally, Christian witnessing means sharing the love of Christ. Perhaps Bonhoeffer has stressed this form of witness more than other contemporary theologians. Our witness in a secular age must take the form of "Christian presence" in addition to Christian preaching. It is not only the evangelical proclamation of the death of Christ but also the demonstration of a Christian life that can be a potent means of grace for secular man. Against the new secular or radical theologians, however, I must insist that a Christian style of life cannot take the place of evangelical kerygmatic preaching.

We must finally recognize that no life, not even that of the greatest saint, can bring men the assurance of forgiveness which they so desperately need. The one thing needful is to wait upon and hear the Word of God, the message of salvation through the shedding of the blood of Jesus Christ. Our lives must reflect and attest this Word, but they will do so only if men have been told about this Word.

* * * * *

The basic issue today is evangelism versus religious imperialism. Religious imperialism has generally taken two forms. The first is apologetics, the attempt to compel a man by rational means to assent to the truth of faith.[5] It is the discipline by which one seeks to persuade or move men by one's own intellectual and moral powers. The other form of religious imperialism is proselytism, the attempt to win people over to a particular theological position or denominational loyalty. It is not so much a ministry to persons as an open bid for recruits. The danger in both of these approaches is that the church may begin trusting in its own power and wisdom rather than in the Word of God and thereby fall into that state of decadence which Barth has called "self-glorification" or "sacralization." There is also the peril of treating our hearers as objects rather than as persons who are claimed by God's love.

The alternative to religious imperialism is Gospel evangelism. Evangelism is not a recruitment program for a particular church but simply confronting men with the Gospel call to decision. The Gospel calls not for the conclusion of the mind but rather the commitment of the self. The herald of the Gospel must take heed neither to patronize nor manipulate his hearers; instead he should seek only to awaken them to the remission of sins and the hope of redemption. His weapons are divine, namely, "the sword of the Spirit," "the Word of God," and "the helmet of salvation." It is with such weapons and not by counter-arguments that we "destroy arguments and every proud obstacle to the knowledge of God" (2 Cor. 10:5).

The object of a truly biblical evangelism is not mutual understanding nor togetherness nor even a higher synthesis but rather unconditional surrender to the God who revealed himself in Jesus Christ. It is the exaltation and glorification of this God which the minister of the Gospel seeks. Even so this is only one side of authentic Christocentric evangelism. The other side is the conversion and liberation of man. Evangelism has for its aim, therefore, not only the service of the glory of God but the salvation of lost men. This is a truth we must never forget, particularly in a time when theologians are speaking about a universal salvation already accomplished by Christ. It is a truth which must also be affirmed against certain secular theologians (such as Paul van Buren, William Hamilton, Howard Moody) who envisage the Christian mission exclusively in terms of *diakonia* and who give no support either to apologetics or to evangelism.[6] The evangelist sees his hearers not as fellow-seekers in the quest for righteousness but as sinners for whom Christ has died. He hopes that they will become children of God, and that they will be adopted into God's family by faith, but he does not assume that they are necessarily already in this family.

This is not to deny that the Holy Spirit works in the world outside the church as well as within the church. Indeed, God does not leave himself without a witness in any culture and race (Acts 14:17). Yet certainly the Spirit of God works in a different way in the secular world than he does in the community of faith. In the world the Spirit restrains the rapacity of men, whereas in the church he liberates men from the dominion of sin. The general providence of God in the world must not be confused with the saving work of Jesus Christ, which is limited to the community of faith.

Historic Calvinism has generally made a distinction between common grace and saving grace pointing to the fact that God accomplishes his purposes in a different way for believers and unbelievers. A contemporary statement on this twofold working of God is given by Clinton Morrison in his book *The Powers That Be.*[7] Morrison distinguishes between the lordship of Christ (which includes the whole world) and the locus of his victory (the church). Karl Barth has challenged this general distinction, but nevertheless it contains the truth that faith is the precondition for service in the kingdom of Christ.

Gospel evangelism is to be contrasted with the "new evangelism" popularized by such men as Colin Williams, John Robinson, and Harvey Cox.[8] These theologians see evangelism primarily in terms of social outreach and involvement in the political issues of the time. The object of evangelism, they maintain, is not the conversion of lost souls but the conversion of outmoded social structures. In their view the attention of the Christian should be focused not on life in eternity but on a new social order in this world. My position is that the Gospel is both radically social and fully personal. Its immediate concern is personal salvation, but its ultimate goal is a holy community. We enter the kingdom one by one, but we immediately find ourselves in the company of the saints who seek to bring the whole world into submission to Jesus Christ. At the same time we have to recognize that all orders and communities in this world will have to perish when God creates his world anew (Bonhoeffer). The kingdom of God lies beyond history even though it is present in germinal form in the community of faith. We can set up signs of the coming kingdom, but we cannot usher in this eschatological reality.

We must now determine whether there is any place at all for apologetics in the theological task today. First of all, it is my view that apologetics as a preparation for and validation of the Gospel is not tenable. Reason is not a springboard to revelation, only a servant of revelation. We are called upon to demonstrate not how the Gospel answers the questions of the culture but how all questions stand under the judgment of the Christian answer. We should not strive to make the Gospel relevant to the secular age, for then the Gospel becomes only another form of the wisdom of this world. Instead we should confront the modern world with the secular relevance already present in the Gospel. In Bonhoeffer's words:

> The intention should be not to justify Christianity in this present age, but *to justify the present age before the Christian message.* Interpretation then means that the present age is brought before the forum of the Christian message, in other words that the question is of the *fact* . . . of the Christian message instead of being of the character of the present age, as in the false concept of relevance.[9]

Still there is an element of truth in the traditional apologetic enterprise which must not be lost. This is the need to take seriously the phenomenon of unbelief and to grapple with attacks upon the faith from the outside world. Yet our purpose should be not to convince the secular man of the superiority of the Christian position over other positions but rather to understand more fully the dichotomy between faith and unbelief. A secondary purpose should be to appreciate the permanently valid insights of secular thought, insights made possible by the *imago Dei* and by common grace.[10] It is then possible for us to extricate such insights from their ideological context and bring them into the service of biblical thinking. Our ultimate aim is not to make our message more palatable to the secular man but rather more lucid and understandable. We should seek an ever deeper understanding of cultural ideology so that we can be certain that what we proclaim is not an ideology but the Gospel.

A certain kind of apologetics, reconceived as a wrestling with unbelief for the purpose of clarifying and understanding faith, is not only possible but mandatory. Such an "apologetics" does not aspire to prove or validate the faith but aims only to clarify the faith in the light of attacks upon it. This is apologetics in the context of faith seeking understanding. The theologian will take the questions of the world seriously, not in order to link these questions with the Christian answer but only in order to understand better both the answer and the question of faith. Karl Barth is profoundly right: "The Church must enter into the questions and movements of the age, but in order, by so doing, to understand anew and to understand better what the true Church is." [11]

There can be only one kind of theology—a biblical dogmatic theology. This theology, though, should have two sides—biblical explication and cultural analysis. The latter, which could better be termed "the theology of culture" or "believing integration" instead of apologetics, aims to help the believer to integrate his faith and experience. This discipline serves evangelism by illumining the situation of our hearers. It also enables us to incarnate our message in the cultural situation. It does this by showing us where to *aim* our fire, not where to *mix* our fire nor where to *draw* our fire.

Apologetics, as I now try to redefine it, is oriented not about a defense of the faith but rather about the heralding and explication of the message of the Bible. It is no longer conceived either as an offensive or a defensive enterprise which tries to prove the superiority of Christianity over other religions or ideologies. Rather it is to be seen as a "confessional enterprise" carried on within the confines of the Christian community. It is that aspect of dogmatic theology which interprets the questions of unbelief in the light of faith. "Apologetics" is no longer a propaedeutic device leading to the sermon, but rather a supplementation of the sermon. If rightly carried out it can serve to illuminate and clarify faith, but it does not give faith its foundation. As Forsyth has rightly declared: "Apologetic is not so valuable to convert the world as to confirm the Church which does convert . . . and to unify its knowledge of the Son of God." [12]

The two main components of an intelligible witness, then, are fidelity to the kerygma and the penetration of the cultural situation. The first concerns the content of our witness; the second has to do with the structure. We need to know secular thought in order to have a clear perception both of the content of our message and how it can be structured or formulated. To be sure the Christian message contravenes rather than corresponds to secular philosophy, but this is precisely the reason why a knowledge of the latter can enable us to understand more fully the meaning of the former. A knowledge of secular culture can help us to distinguish the truth of faith from its past theological expressions which are invariably partly culturally conditioned. It can aid us in determining which secular concepts and symbols lend themselves to theological appropriation and which carry with them too great a risk of ideological contamination. It can enable us to formulate our message in such a way that it represents the mind of Christ and not the bias of the culture.

A theological investigation of secular culture will acquaint us with the thought world of our time so that we can communicate intelligibly and persuasively. It will make it possible for us to discern the flaws in the criticisms of our opponents and thereby strengthen us in our perception and appreciation of the truth of the Christian position.

In this sense a "theology of the secular," understood as a critical analysis of secular thought in the light of divine revelation, is the substitute for traditional apologetics. Moreover, such a discipline will enable us to speak in the language of the culture and at the same time utilize this language in the service of a truth which stands in judgment over the culture. It can also help us to understand the burning social issues of the time so that we can speak relevantly and prophetically. Indeed, how can we preach the full Gospel without relating it to the nuclear armaments race, the population explosion, or the racial crisis?

In summary, a theology which takes Scripture as its basic authority will be kerygmatic and confessional in orientation rather than apologetic (in the traditional sense). In other words, it will seek to reach the world outside the church primarily by means of evangelical proclamation rather than argument in defense of the faith.

For the kerygmatic theologian the point of contact with secular culture, as with any pagan culture, can be neither the questions nor the strivings of that culture; the point of contact is none other than the Holy Spirit who converts and transforms the searchings and strivings of the natural man. Against Niebuhr, for example, we maintain that it is useless to appeal to man's uneasy conscience, since the wicked are "always at ease" and have stifled the voice of their conscience (cf. Ps. 73:12; Amos 6:1). Our appeal should be directed to the Spirit of God, who alone can penetrate the hardened hearts of sinners (cf. John 16:8). As Paul declared, "No one can say 'Jesus is Lord' except by the Holy Spirit" (1 Cor. 12:3). Indeed it is only the Holy Spirit who can tear out the root of bitterness which blinds us to our true condition. It is only the Spirit who can shatter the iron doors of the prison of egocentricity in which we find ourselves (cf. Ps. 107:16; Is. 45:2). It is when we are confronted by the Spirit that our conscience is stricken and we are impelled to seek the truth that can make us free.

The theology I propose is not purely kerygmatic, however, since the witness of the Christian life must also be taken into consideration. Indeed, in our present age there is an acute need not only for an intelligible oral witness but also for a Christian style of life, a life arrayed against the values of the secular man. This is the abiding truth in Pietism and Puritanism, a truth also recognized by many of the students of Bonhoeffer. This Christian style of life cannot be a substitute for the evangelical proclamation, but it can be a powerful support for this proclamation, for the Holy Spirit acts not only through the word of preaching but also through deeds of mercy (cf. Matt. 5:16; Rom. 15:18, 2 Cor. 3:2, 3; 1 Peter 2:12, 3:1, 2). In a time when the demons are venting their fury against the church of Jesus Christ, the Christian needs to put on the whole armor of God, including the shield of a holy life as well as the sword of the Spirit, which is the Word of God. A theology of proclamation needs to be supplemented by a theology of devotion if the church is to maintain itself in a secular age.[13]

Notes

I.

INTRODUCTION: THE SECULARIZATION OF WESTERN CULTURE

1. In this book the term "modern age" refers to the new age of scientific discovery and accomplishment, beginning with the Enlightenment and continuing in the present. The term "post-modern age" refers to the period of despair and disillusionment which followed the first world war and in which we still find ourselves. It is an age within an age, or perhaps an age which marks the transition from one period of history to another.
2. Marc Boegner, a former president of the World Council of Churches, gives an able statement on what the term "post-Christian" means as it is applied to the present age: "One fact is immediately plain: What has been called Christianity has ceased to exist—not only because the political structure of most states and their conscious or unconscious philosophy forbid calling them Christian; not only because the division of the church into a multiplicity of denominations is contrary to the very idea of Christianity; but even more because our time is marked by the dechristianization of nations which through long centuries declared that they were Christian. . . . Today we cannot and ought not to speak of a Christian humanism—unless indeed to evoke a distant memory or express a hope. The humanism of this era of ours is atheistic (though it may mask its atheism) and in even greater degree anti-Christian. There are no longer any Christian nations; there are only Christians—larger or smaller numbers of them in more or less separate groups—in a western Europe that has in great part become pagan again." Marc Boegner, "After Christianity—What?" in *The Christian Century,* Vol. LXVII (March 7, 1951), p. 297.
3. Harnack contends that despite the church's rejection of Gnosticism, the gradual blending with Hellenistic philosophy during the first few centuries made possible by the work of the apologists amounted to a very similar distortion of the faith. Harnack distinguishes between Gnosticism and Catholicism: "The great distinction here consists essentially in the fact that the Gnostic systems represent the acute secularising or hellenising of Christianity, with the rejection of the Old Testament, while the Catholic system, on the other hand, represents a gradual process of the same kind with the conservation of the Old Testament. The traditional religion on

being, as it were, suddenly required to recognize itself in a picture foreign to it, was yet vigorous enough to reject that picture; but to the gradual, one might say indulgent remodelling to which it was subjected, it offered but little resistance, nay, as a rule, it was never conscious of it. It is therefore no paradox to say that Gnosticism, which is just Hellenism, has in Catholicism obtained half a victory." Adolf Harnack, *History of Dogma,* Vol. I, trans. from 3rd German edition by Neil Buchanan (New York, Russell & Russell, 1958), pp. 226-227.

4. *Ibid.,* Vol. II, p. 228.
5. Irenaeus, *Irenaeus Against Heresies* in *The Ante-Nicene Fathers,* Vol. I. Eds. Alexander Roberts and James Donaldson (N.Y., Charles Scribner's Sons, 1926), p. 418. Irenaeus points out that Jesus never addressed his hearers, including his disciples, according to their preconceived notions: "He therefore did not address them in accordance with their pristine notions, nor did He reply to them in harmony with the opinion of His questioners, but according to the doctrine leading to salvation, without hypocrisy or respect of person."
6. Tertullian, *On Prescription Against Heretics,* in *The Ante-Nicene Fathers,* Vol. III, p. 246.
7. Forsyth writes concerning the conflict of the early church with Gnosticism: "And what was it that then saved the Church for the future and for the Gospel? It was not the apologists nor the line they took in presenting Christianity as the noblest of all the cultures, the most comprehensive of all the philosophies. . . . That was a line that developed the gnostic tendency, as it is the leading line in the gnosticism of today. But the situation was saved by the other line, by Athanasius, who developed everything that distinguished his position out of the principle of the experienced redemption of a ruined world. To express this unutterable reality he had to do as Paul did, to capture and transform the speculation of the day; and he had even to coin a new metaphysic. He converted the past more than he developed it. He descended on the world, like the true preacher he was, rather than arose from it. . . . He compelled the world to accommodate itself to him by preserving an evangelical isolation from it." P. T. Forsyth, *Positive Preaching and the Modern Mind* (London, Independent Press, 1953), pp. 79, 80.
8. For a penetrating discussion of how the theology of Augustine and Aquinas compromised the biblical idea of Agape by amalgamating it with the Platonic idea of Eros, see Anders Nygren, *Agape and Eros,* translated by Philip Watson (Philadelphia, Westminster Press, 1953).
9. John Locke, *An Essay Concerning Understanding,* Vol. II (N.Y., Dover Publications, Inc., 1950), p. 438.
10. Edward Herbert of Cherbury enumerated some of these axioms, including the following: God exists; He is to be worshiped; virtue is his true service; man must repent of wrong doing; there are rewards and punishments after death. The later Deists raised doubts concerning even these notions.
11. The modern (or what we prefer to call the post-modern) temper is certainly mirrored in the following statement: "Skepticism has entered too

deeply into our souls ever to be replaced by faith, and we can never forget the things which the new barbarians will never need to have known. This world in which an unresolvable discord is the fundamental fact is the world in which we must continue to live, and for us wisdom must consist, not in searching for a means of escape which does not exist, but in making such peace with it as we may. . . . If death for us and our kind is the inevitable result of our stubbornness then we can only say, 'So be it.' Ours is a lost cause and there is no place for us in the natural universe, but we are not, for all that, sorry to be human. We should rather die as men than live as animals." Joseph Wood Krutch, *The Modern Temper* (N.Y., Harcourt, Brace & Co., 1931), pp. 247, 249.

12. Emil Brunner, *Christianity and Civilization,* Vol. II (N.Y., Charles Scribner's Sons, 1949), p. 24.
13. See his essay, "The Place of Christianity Among the World Religions" in Ernst Troeltsch, *Christian Thought: Its History and Application,* Ed. Baron von Huegel (N.Y., Meridian Books, 1957), pp. 34-63.
14. See his essay, "The Idea of God and Modern Man" in Rudolf Bultmann, *et al. Translating Theology into the Modern Age* (N.Y., Harper Torchbooks, 1965), pp. 83-95.
15. Other theologians who can be placed in the camp of the new secular or radical theology are Gibson Winter, Thomas Altizer, Herbert Braun, Leslie Dewart, Ernest Harrison, R. Gregor Smith, Malcolm Boyd, James Pike, Colin Williams, Howard Moody, Richard Rubenstein and Stephen Rose. It must be recognized that the category of radical theology embraces various theological positions. Only Altizer, van Buren, William Hamilton, Rubenstein, and Harrison can be classified as death-of-God theologians.

II.

REAPPRAISING THE CHRISTIAN WITNESS

1. Karl Barth rightly points out that the world has always been secular, and this was true even in the Middle Ages. Yet when the church becomes secular, when it becomes a cultural or national church, then it is threatened with inner decomposition. Karl Barth, *Church Dogmatics,* Vol. IV, 2nd ed., G. W. Bromiley & T. F. Torrance, trans G. W. Bromiley (Edinburgh, T. & T. Clark, 1958), p. 668.
2. In technical usage apologetics refers to the attempt to instruct Christians on how they can best answer attacks upon the Christian faith from the outside world. An apology is a specific answer to a direct attack upon the faith, an answer directed to the outsider or the non-Christian.
3. Paul's address on Mars Hill (Acts 17:22-34) is sometimes cited as an example of an apologia in the New Testament. Barth maintains that Paul was simply expounding upon the creation viewed in the light of the resurrection. Whatever Paul's intentions it cannot be doubted that he had second thoughts on the efficacy of this particular method. When he went to

Corinth he resolved to know nothing except Jesus and him crucified (1 Cor. 2:1-5). It seems that his mission in Athens bore no lasting fruit, since in 1 Cor. 16:15 he refers to the household of Stephanas in Corinth and not to the Athenians as "the first converts in Achaia."

4. From Luther's *Fastenpostille.* Quoted in Karl Barth, *Church Dogmatics,* I, 1, trans. G. T. Thomson (Edinburgh, T. & T. Clark, 1949), p. 33 n.
5. John Calvin, *Institutes of the Christian Religion,* I, 7, 2, trans. John Allen, 7th American ed. (Philadelphia, Presbyterian Board of Christian Education, 1936), p. 89.
6. Søren Kierkegaard, *Concluding Unscientific Postscript,* trans. David Swenson (Princeton, Princeton University Press, 1944), p. 343.
7. Søren Kierkegaard, *On Authority and Revelation,* trans. Walter Lowrie (Princeton, Princeton University Press, 1955), p. 59.
8. Søren Kierkegaard, *The Journals of Søren Kierkegaard,* trans. Alexander Dru, 2nd ed. (London, Oxford University Press, 1951), p. 259.
9. Emil Brunner, *Revelation and Reason,* trans. Olive Wyon (Philadelphia, Westminster Press, 1946), p. 212.
10. See his book *Reasons for Faith* (N.Y., Harper & Bros., 1960). This is not to deny Dr. Gerstner's very solid contributions in some other areas, e.g., the history of theology.
11. Even Paul van Buren, who addresses himself to the community of faith rather than to the world outside the church, is motivated by the desire to make the faith meaningful to the modern secular mind. For a poignant critique of van Buren's position see Kenneth Hamilton, *Revolt Against Heaven* (Grand Rapids, Eerdmans, 1965), pp. 157-165. Also see E. L. Mascall, *The Secularization of Christianity* (N.Y., Holt, Rinehart & Winston, 1966), pp. 40-105.
12. Dietrich Bonhoeffer, *Letters and Papers from Prison,* ed. Eberhard Bethge, trans. Reginald Fuller (N.Y., Macmillan Co., 1953), p. 235.
13. Karl Barth, *Evangelical Theology: An Introduction,* trans. Grover Foley (Garden City, N.Y., Doubleday & Co., Inc., 1964), p. 11.
14. *Ibid.,* pp. 161, 162.

III.

KARL BARTH

1. Karl Barth, *Dogmatics in Outline,* trans. G. T. Thomson (N.Y., Philosophical Library, n.d.), p. 26.
2. Karl Barth, *Church Dogmatics,* II, 1, eds. G. W. Bromiley and T. F. Torrance, trans. T. H. Parker, *et al.* (Edinburgh, T. & T. Clark, 1957), p. 13.
3. In Barth's theology God speaks not in and through but only with, over, and against human activity. He writes: "God's action never takes place 'in and under.' It certainly takes place 'with' man's activity, but also above and in face of it." *Church Dogmatics,* III, 4, trans. T. H. Parker *et al.* (Edinburgh, T. & T. Clark, 1961), p. 521. This is why he maintains that

it is impossible for man to preach the Word of God. The most that man can hope for is that God's Word might also be active in conjunction with his preaching.

4. Karl Barth, *Church Dogmatics,* IV, 1, p. 775.
5. Karl Barth, *Karl Barth's Table Talk,* ed. John D. Godsey (Edinburgh, Oliver and Boyd, 1963), p. 87.
6. Karl Barth, *Against the Stream* (London, SCM Press, Ltd., 1954), p. 216.
7. Barth writes: "It is a bad sign when Christians are frightened by 'political' sermons—as if Christian preaching could be anything but political. And if it were not political, how would it show that it is the salt and the light of the world?" Karl Barth, *Community, State and Church* (Garden City, N.Y., Doubleday & Co., 1960), p. 185.
8. Barth, *Church Dogmatics.* IV, 3, b, p. 891.
9. Barth has written: "On the basis of the eternal will of God we have to think of *every human being* . . . as one to whom Jesus Christ is Brother and God is Father; and we have to deal with him on this assumption. If the other person knows that already, then we have to strengthen him in the knowledge. If he does not know it yet or no longer knows it, our business is to transmit this knowledge to him." Karl Barth, *The Humanity of God* (Richmond, Va., John Knox Press, 1964), p. 53.
10. *Ibid.,* pp. 58, 59. Barth at the same time maintains that in one sense even Christians are outsiders in that they continue to sin and thereby fall short of the glory of God.
11. Barth, *Church Dogmatics,* IV, 3, a, p. 117.
12. Brunner says that in Barth's theology the unbelieving world might be likened to people who only seem to be perishing in a stormy sea. But in reality they are not in a sea at all but in shallow water where it is impossible for them to drown. Their plight is that they do not recognize that there is no danger. Emil Brunner, *The Christian Doctrine of God,* trans. Olive Wyon (Philadelphia, Westminster Press, 1950), p. 351.
13. Barth, *Church Dogmatics,* IV, 3, b, p. 852.

IV.
EMIL BRUNNER

1. Emil Brunner, "Towards a Missionary Theology" in *The Christian Century* (July 6, 1949), p. 817.
2. See Emil Brunner, "Nature and Grace" in *Natural Theology,* trans. Peter Fraenkel (London, Centenary Press, 1946).
3. Emil Brunner, *Eternal Hope,* trans. Harold Knight (Philadelphia, Westminster Press, 1954), p. 212.
4. Emil Brunner, *The Christian Doctrine of Creation and Redemption,* trans. Olive Wyon (Philadelphia, Westminster Press, 1952), p. 23.

5. See Martin Heidegger, *An Introduction to Metaphysics,* trans. Ralph Manheim (Garden City, N.Y., Doubleday & Co., Inc., Anchor Books, 1961), p. 6.
6. In Charles Kegley, ed., *The Theology of Emil Brunner* (N.Y., Macmillan Co., 1962), p. 183.
7. Bonhoeffer writes: " . . . the Christian person achieves his true nature when God does not confront him as Thou, but 'enters into' him as I." Dietrich Bonhoeffer, *The Communion of Saints,* trans. R. Gregor Smith (N.Y., Harper & Row, 1963), p. 37.
8. Emil Brunner, *Truth as Encounter,* trans. Amandus Loos and David Cairns (Philadelphia, Westminster Press, 1964), p. 49.
9. Emil Brunner, *The Christian Doctrine of Creation and Redemption,* p. 72.
10. See Emil Brunner, *Man in Revolt,* trans. Olive Wyon (N.Y., Charles Scribner's Sons, 1939), p. 174.
11. Emil Brunner, *The Mediator,* trans. Olive Wyon (London, Lutterworth Press, 1949), p. 600; cf. his *The Philosophy of Religion,* trans. A. J. D. Farrar and Bertram Lee Woolf (London) James Clarke & Co. Ltd., 1958), p. 78.
12. Emil Brunner, *Revelation and Reason,* trans. Olive Wyon (Philadelphia, Westminster Press, 1956), pp. 6, 7.
13. *Ibid.,* p. 201. Cf. his *The Christian Doctrine of God,* trans. Olive Wyon (Philadelphia, Westminster Press, 1950), p. 35.
14. Emil Brunner, *The Church in the New Social Order* (London, SCM Press Ltd., 1952), p. 7.

V.

RUDOLF BULTMANN

1. Rudolf Bultmann, "A Reply to the Theses of J. Schniewind," in *Kerygma and Myth,* I, ed. Hans W. Bartsch, trans. Reginald Fuller (London, S.P.C.K., 1960), p. 123.
2. According to Reginald Fuller the "Christ event" or the "eschatological event" in Bultmann's theology comprises the cross plus the preaching of the kerygma plus the acceptance of the preaching in faith. Reginald Fuller, *The New Testament in Current Study* (N.Y., Charles Scribner's Sons, 1962), pp. 14, 15.
3. Rudolf Bultmann, "The Case for Demythologizing," in *Kerygma and Myth,* II, ed. Hans-Werner Bartsch, trans. R. H. Fuller (London, S.P.C.K., 1962), pp. 182, 183.
4. *Ibid.,* p. 192. He has also written: ". . . the depths of divine love are opened out only to him who allows himself to be emancipated from his attachment to the things of time and space and who allows Christ to effect this redemptive work of emancipation in his life." R. Bultmann, *This World and the Beyond,* trans. Harold Knight (London, Lutterworth Press, 1960), p. 142.

5. Rudolf Bultmann, "New Testament and Mythology," in *Kerygma and Myth,* I, p. 10. It can be seen that Bultmann has accepted the definition of myth which has been present in the History of Religions School.
6. *Ibid.,* p. 197.
7. Schubert Ogden, who seeks to incorporate existentialist insights into a process philosophy, fails to do justice to the eternal significance and uniqueness of Jesus Christ. In his book *Christ Without Myth* (N.Y., Harper & Row, 1961) he disputes the idea that Christ performed a cosmic work of redemption. For him Jesus is simply a decisive manifestation of that primordial love which makes authentic life possible (pp. 132 f., 142 f.). Salvation consists essentially in the realization of authentic existence which is a universal or ever present possibility.

   Bultmann is much more insistent than Ogden upon the need for a personal encounter with the Christ proclaimed by the church. Yet even he has declared: "It would be false to deny that the 'possibility in principle'—which I in fact do not contest—could become a 'possibility in fact' without faith in Jesus Christ as the decisive act of God. God's liberating act may occur everywhere, even if at the same time it is decisively revealed in the Word which Jesus speaks and which he is." Charles W. Kegley, ed., *The Theology of Rudolf Bultmann* (N.Y., Harper & Row, 1966), p. 272.
8. The revelational myth might aptly be called a saga (a term Barth uses) in that it is a poetic picture of divine action in history rather than a symbolic description of a timeless truth. The stories of the creation, fall, resurrection, and ascension can all be considered sacred sagas. It must be acknowledged that there are mythical elements in the pagan sense still present in the Bible, but they have been subordinated to the dominant themes of historical revelation. For a helpful discussion of the relation between myth and revelation, see Avery Dulles, "Symbol, Myth, and the Biblical Revelation" in *New Theology No. 4,* eds. Martin Marty and Dean Peerman (N.Y., Macmillan, 1967), pp. 39-68.
9. Barth rightly poses the question: " . . . it may be asked whether it is right to stigmatize everything mythological as though it were *ipso facto* absolutely useless for modern man. Why should not the divine be described in terms of human life, the other-worldly in terms of this world, the non-objective as objective?" Karl Barth, "Rudolf Bultmann—An Attempt to Understand Him," in *Kerygma and Myth, II,* p. 108.
10. Regin Prenter, "Myth and Gospel" in Carl Braaten and Roy Harrisville, eds. and trans., *Kerygma and History* (N.Y., Abingdon Press, 1962), pp. 136, 137.
11. Rudolf Bultmann, "A Reply to the Theses of J. Schniewind," in *Kerygma and Myth,* I, p. 107.
12. Fritz Buri of the University of Basel, who leans heavily on Bultmann, seeks to go still further and "dekerygmatize" biblical faith.
13. Rudolf Bultmann, *Glauben und Verstehen* (Tuebingen, Verlag Von J. C. B. Mohr, 1933), p. 311.
14. Rudolf Bultmann, *et al., Translating Theology Into the Modern Age,* ed.

Robert Funk, trans. Charles Carlston, *et al.* (N.Y., Harper & Row, 1965), p. 94.

15. Rudolf Bultmann, *Jesus Christ and Mythology* (N.Y., Charles Scribner's Sons, 1958), p. 38.
16. I am not suggesting that all men are saved, but that even in their self-condemnation they are upheld by the grace assured to us by the death and resurrection of Jesus Christ.

VI.

REINHOLD NIEBUHR

1. The Evangelical Synod, to which Niebuhr belonged, later merged with the German Reformed Church to form the Evangelical and Reformed Church. This denomination now forms a part of the United Church of Christ.
2. Reinhold Niebuhr, *Does Civilization Need Religion?* (N.Y., Macmillan Co., 1927), p. 15.
3. Reinhold Niebuhr, "The Preaching of Repentance" in *The Christian Century* (June 18, 1930), p. 781.
4. This idea is more fully developed in his *The Nature and Destiny of Man,* Vol. II (N.Y., Charles Scribner's Sons, 1943), pp. 289 f.
5. See his article "The Truth in Myths" in Julius S. Bixler, ed., *The Nature of Religious Experience,* (N.Y., Harper & Bros., 1937), pp. 117-135.
6. Reinhold Niebuhr, *The Nature and Destiny of Man,* Vol. I (N.Y., Charles Scribner's Sons, 1941), p. 127.
7. Reinhold Niebuhr, *Leaves from the Notebook of a Tamed Cynic* (Chicago, Willett, Clark & Colby, 1929), p. 41.
8. Reinhold Niebuhr, *Faith and History* (N.Y., Charles Scribner's Sons, 1949,) p. 167.
9. Niebuhr maintains that modern Socratic culture has not stated the questions for which Christ is the answer. But now with the breakup of modern culture men are once more seeking for fulfillment beyond themselves, and the Christian faith has again become a live option for men.
10. Reinhold Niebuhr, *The Nature and Destiny of Man,* Vol. II (N.Y., Charles Scribner's Sons, 1943), pp. 206, 207.
11. In a recent work he maintains that the basis of Christian realism is the belief "that human nature contains both self-regarding and social impulses and that the former is stronger than the latter." Reinhold Niebuhr, *Man's Nature and His Communities* (N.Y., Charles Scribner's Sons, 1965), p. 39. In this book he also seeks to do justice to the abiding truth in Christian idealism.
12. In a significant article written in 1954 Niebuhr maintains that the Christian witness must take the form of soberness and watchfulness as over against the direct proclamation of a personal hope in the resurrection of

Jesus Christ. See his "Christ the Hope of the World" in *Religion in Life,* (Summer, 1954), pp. 334-340.

13. Reinhold Niebuhr, *The Nature and Destiny of Man,* Vol. I, p. 266.
14. Reinhold Niebuhr, *Faith and History,* p. 26.
15. John Cogley, "An Interview With Reinhold Niebuhr" in *McCall's* (Feb., 1966), p. 171. It is interesting to note that already at the beginning of his theological career Niebuhr was insisting that there can be nothing absolute in history no matter how frequently God may intervene in it. See his "Must We Do Nothing?" in *The Christian Century* (March 30, 1932), pp. 415-417.
16. Niebuhr maintains that the revelation of the cross of Christ does not superimpose but rather clarifies the truth about man's situation. It does not create a new norm but illuminates the norm already given by the very constitution of selfhood. Reinhold Niebuhr, *The Self and the Dramas of History* (N.Y., Charles Scribner's Sons, 1955), p. 232.
17. See his book *The Children of Light and the Children of Darkness* (N.Y., Charles Scribner's Sons, 1944).
18. See Charles W. Kegley and Robert W. Bretall, eds., *Reinhold Niebuhr: His Religious, Social, and Political Thought* (N.Y., Macmillan Co., 1956) pp. 225-228.
19. Reinhold Niebuhr, "The Crisis in American Protestantism" in *The Christian Century* (Dec. 4, 1963), p. 1501.

VII.
PAUL TILLICH

1. Paul Tillich, *The Protestant Era,* trans. James Luther Adams (Chicago, University of Chicago Press, 1948), p. 229.
2. *Ibid.,* p. 262.
3. Paul Tillich, *Ultimate Concern,* ed. D. M. Brown (N.Y., Harper & Row, 1965), pp. 88, 89.
4. Paul Tillich, "Symbol and Knowledge: A Reply" in *The Journal of Liberal Religion* (Spring, 1941), p. 204.
5. See Paul Tillich, "What is Wrong with the 'Dialectic' Theology" in *The Journal of Religion* (April, 1935), pp. 127-145.
6. Paul Tillich, "The Present Theological Situation in the Light of the Continental European Development," *Theology Today* (Oct., 1949), p. 305.
7. Paul Tillich, *The Protestant Era,* p. 203.
8. He declares: " . . . the decision for or against Christ is made by people who do not even know his name. What is decisive is only whether they act for or against the law of love, for which Christ stands." Paul Tillich, *Biblical Religion and the Search for Ultimate Reality* (Chicago, University of Chicago Press, 1955), p. 46.

9. Paul Tillich, *Systematic Theology,* Vol. II (Chicago, University of Chicago Press, 1957), pp. 101-118.
10. See Robert Johnson, *Authority in Protestant Theology* (Philadelphia, Westminster Press, 1959), pp. 111-143.
11. See James Luther Adams, *Paul Tillich's Philosophy of Culture, Science, and Religion* (N.Y., Harper & Row, 1965), p. 32. Other philosophers who have influenced Tillich and which are mentioned by Adams are Schelling, Kant, Husserl, and Kierkegaard.
12. Paul Tillich, *Systematic Theology,* Vol. I, p. 94.
13. The dichotomy between God and man is underscored in the following passage from one of Tillich's sermons: "Whenever the Divine appears, It is a radical attack on everything that is good in man, and therefore man must repel It, must push It away, must crucify It. Whenever the Divine manifests Itself as the new reality, It must be rejected by the representatives of the old reality. For the Divine does not complete the human; It revolts against the human. Because of that, the human must defend itself against It, must reject It, and must try to destroy It." Paul Tillich, *The Shaking of the Foundations* (N.Y., Charles Scribner's Sons, 1952,) p. 147.
14. Karl Barth, *Church Dogmatics,* Vol. II, eds. G. W. Bromiley and T. F. Torrance, trans. G. W. Bromiley, *et al.* (Edinburgh: T. & T. Clark, 1957), p. 257.
15. Pascal's interpretation is certainly in accord with the biblical witness: "Not only do we know God by Jesus Christ alone, but we know ourselves only by Jesus Christ. We know life and death only through Jesus Christ. Apart from Jesus Christ, we do not know what is our life, nor our death, nor God, nor ourselves." Blaise Pascal, *Pensées and the Provincial Letters* (N.Y., Modern Library, Random House, 1941), p. 173.
16. Paul Tillich, *Systematic Theology.* Vol. III (Chicago, University of Chicago Press, 1963), p. 220.
17. Paul Tillich, *Systematic Theology,* Vol. I, p. 155.

VIII.
DIETRICH BONHOEFFER

1. Eberhard Bethge, "The Challenge of Dietrich Bonhoeffer's Life and Theology" in *The Chicago Theological Seminary Register* (Feb., 1961), p. 8.
2. Dietrich Bonhoeffer, *Act and Being,* trans. Bernard Noble (N.Y., Harper & Bros., 1956), p. 89.
3. Already in his *Nachfolge* Bonhoeffer is deeply critical of apologetics: "They [Christians] are simply servants and instruments of the Word: they have no wish to be strong where the Word chooses to be weak. To try and

force the Word on the world by hook or by crook is to make the living Word of God into a mere idea, and the world would be perfectly justified in refusing to listen to an idea for which it had no use." Dietrich Bonhoeffer, *The Cost of Discipleship,* trans. R. H. Fuller (London, SCM Press, Ltd., 1959), p. 166.

4. Kenneth Hamilton maintains that Bonhoeffer basically remains within the supernaturalist camp despite his search for a nonreligious interpretation of the faith. See Hamilton, *Revolt Against Heaven* (Grand Rapids, Wm. B. Eerdmans, 1965), pp. 169-180. This book can be recommended as an enlightening introduction to modern theology.
5. Bonhoeffer regards the Chalcedonian formula not as metaphysical speculation but as a testimony to the Godmanhood of Jesus Christ in the language of symbol and paradox. His Christology excludes the doctrine of the two natures, but he holds that the Chalcedonian definition actually superseded this doctrine. See his *Christ the Center* (N.Y., Harper & Row, 1966), pp. 91, 92, 101.
6. Dietrich Bonhoeffer, *Letters and Papers from Prison,* ed. Eberhard Bethge, trans. Reginald Fuller (N.Y., Macmillan Co., 1953), p. 166.
7. *Ibid.,* pp. 237, 238.
8. In his essay "Thy Kingdom Come," written in 1932, he contends: "The kingdom of God is not to be found in some other world beyond, but in the midst of this world. . . . Even then there will be a kingdom of God on earth, on the new earth of the promise, on the old earth of the creation." John D. Godsey, ed., *Preface to Bonhoeffer* (Philadelphia, Fortress Press, 1965), p. 45.
9. Bonhoeffer's understanding of religion is given this interpretation by van Buren: "This summarizes the characteristics of religion, as Bonhoeffer saw them: thinking of two spheres of reality, the natural and the supernatural; interest in the other-worldly; metaphysical thinking; an idea of transcendence which surpasses human possibilities." Paul van Buren, *The Secular Meaning of the Gospel* (N.Y., Macmillan Co., 1963), p. 82.
10. In his essay "Thy Kingdom Come" (published in 1932) he writes: "Now other-worldliness and secularism are only two sides of the same thing, namely, disbelief in God's kingdom. They disbelieve who would flee the world to reach it, seeking it in a place removed from all their troubles; and they also disbelieve who suppose that they are to erect it themselves as a kingdom of this world." John Godsey, ed., *Preface to Bonhoeffer,* p. 31. He later becomes more appreciative of secularism, but he never espouses a godless Christianity as have some of his latter-day disciples.
11. Dietrich Bonhoeffer, *Letters and Papers from Prison,* p. 224.
12. Reinhold Niebuhr, *The Children of Light and the Children of Darkness* (N.Y., Charles Scribner's Sons, 1944), pp. 131-134.
13. Dietrich Bonhoeffer, *Letters and Papers from Prison,* pp. 226, 227.
14. Dietrich Bonhoeffer, *Ethics,* ed. Eberhard Bethge, trans. Neville Horton Smith (New York, Macmillan Co., 1955), p. 182.

IX.

JOHN ROBINSON

1. David Edwards, ed., *The Honest to God Debate* (Philadelphia, Westminster Press, 1963), p. 279.
2. John A. T. Robinson, *In the End, God . . .*, 2nd ed. (London, James Clarke & Co., Ltd., 1958), p. 24.
3. David Edwards, ed., *The Honest to God Debate,* p. 275.
4. John A. T. Robinson, *Christian Morals Today* (London, SCM Press Ltd., 1964), p. 37.
5. *Ibid.,* p. 42.
6. John A. T. Robinson, *Honest to God* (Philadelphia, Westminster Press, 1963), p. 97.
7. John A. T. Robinson, *Exploration into God* (Stanford, California, Stanford University Press, 1967), p. 139.
8. John A. T. Robinson, *The New Reformation?* (Philadelphia, Westminster Press, 1965), p. 52.
9. Martin E. Marty, "The Bishop and the Debate" in *The Christian Century* (June 24, 1964), p. 832.
10. John A. T. Robinson, *Honest to God,* p. 50.
11. David Edwards, ed., *The Honest to God Debate,* p. 92.
12. John A. T. Robinson, *Exploration into God,* pp. 89-96, 117-118, 160-161.
13. That Robinson's apologetic motif leads him to question the idea of a personal God can be seen in this statement: "If the only alternative to a personal God is a less than personal Absolute, then let us by all means retain the former. Yet it is impossible to escape the fact that this is a serious obstacle to faith for modern secular man, as, indeed, it has always been for Oriental religious man." *Ibid.,* p. 150.
14. This note can also be discerned in his *But That I Can't Believe!* (N.Y., New American Library, 1967), pp. 92-98, 153-158.
15. John A. T. Robinson, *The New Reformation?* p. 41.
16. David Edwards, ed., *The Honest to God Debate,* p. 231.

X.

HARVEY COX

1. Harvey Cox, *God's Revolution and Man's Responsibility* (Valley Forge, Pa., Judson Press, 1965), p. 119.
2. Cox in his book *The Secular City* speaks favorably of Winter and even subscribes to the latter's reinterpretation of prophetic proclamation as "theological reflection" upon the meaning of contemporary events. Cox has a preference for the term "reflection-in-action." *The Secular City* (N.Y., Macmillan Co., 1965), pp. 254-255.

3. Harvey Cox, *On Not Leaving It to the Snake* (N.Y., Macmillan Co., 1967), p. 139.
4. Harvey Cox, *God's Revolution and Man's Responsibility,* pp. 77 f.
5. *Ibid.,* p. 126.
6. Harvey Cox, *The Secular City,* p. 130.
7. Daniel Callahan, ed., *The Secular City Debate* (N.Y., Macmillan Co., 1966), p. 180.
8. *Ibid.,* p. 179.
9. Harvey Cox, *On Not Leaving It to the Snake,* p. 88.
10. That Cox's methodology is basically similar to that of Paul Tillich is also asserted by George Kehm in his "An Excursion in Theological Exorcism" in *McCormick Quarterly* (March, 1966), pp. 240-246.
11. Harvey Cox, *On Not Leaving It to the Snake,* p. 94.
12. Harvey Cox, *The Secular City,* p. 254.
13. Harvey Cox, "The Place and Purpose of Theology" in *The Christian Century* (Jan. 5, 1966), p. 8.
14. *Ibid.*
15. Harvey Cox, *The Secular City,* p. 255.
16. Harvey Cox, *On Not Leaving It to the Snake,* pp. 119, 120.
17. Dietrich Bonhoeffer, *Letters and Papers from Prison,* pp. 187, 188.

XI.

THOMAS ALTIZER

1. Thomas Altizer, *The Gospel of Christian Atheism* (Philadelphia, Westminster Press, 1966), p. 22.
2. *Ibid.,* p. 133.
3. Richard Rubenstein is a marked exception, since his philosophy is much more pessimistic. See his *After Auschwitz* (Indianapolis, Bobbs-Merrill Co., 1966).
4. Altizer, *The Gospel of Christian Atheism,* p. 122.
5. Thomas Altizer and William Hamilton, *Radical Theology and the Death of God* (Indianapolis, Bobbs-Merrill Co., 1966), p. 165.
6. See Paul van Buren, *The Secular Meaning of the Gospel* (N.Y., Macmillan Co., 1963).
7. Altizer, *Radical Theology and the Death of God,* p. 99.
8. See Thomas Altizer, *The New Apocalypse: The Radical Christian Vision of William Blake* (East Lansing, Mich., Mich. State University Press, 1967).
9. Thomas Altizer, *Mircea Eliade and the Dialectic of the Sacred* (Philadelphia, Westminster Press, 1963), p. 200.
10. See Thomas Altizer, *Oriental Mysticism and Biblical Eschatology* (Philadelphia, Westminster Press, 1961).

11. In William Braden, *The Private Sea* (Chicago, Quadrangle Books, 1967). p. 169.
12. Kenneth Hamilton, *God Is Dead* (Grand Rapids, Wm. B. Eerdmans Publishing Co., 1966), pp. 68 f.
13. Altizer, *The Gospel of Christian Atheism,* p. 140.
14. *Ibid.,* p. 145.
15. *Ibid.*
16. *Ibid.,* p. 105.
17. See his "Creative Negation in Theology" in *The Christian Century,* LXXXII, No. 27 (July 7, 1965), p. 866. In this article Altizer champions "Tillich's call for theological contemporaneity."
18. Altizer, *The Gospel of Christian Atheism,* p. 31.
19. *Ibid.,* p. 155.
20. Altizer writes that the theologian is "called to the task of identifying the deepest worldliness of the world as a manifestation of faith and of seeking to engraft that worldliness into the existing forms of faith." Thomas Altizer, "Theology's Response to the Challenge of Secularism." *The Centennial Review* (Vol. XI, No. 4, Fall, 1967), p. 481.
21. Altizer and Hamilton, *Radical Theology and the Death of God,* p. ix.
22. William Hamilton, "The Death of God," in *Playboy* (Aug., 1966), p. 139.
23. Altizer, *Radical Theology and the Death of God,* p. 180.
24. *Ibid.,* p. 184.
25. Nietzsche was not a sensualist in the strict sense; for him it is not animal lust so much as the will to power which is the key to authentic existence.
26. Altizer, *The Gospel of Christian Atheism,* p. 128.
27. William Braden, *The Private Sea,* p. 128.
28. *Ibid.,* pp. 155-177.
29. See Martin Buber, *Eclipse of God* (New York, Harper Torch Books, 1957).

XII.
BEYOND APOLOGETICS: A RESTATEMENT OF THE CHRISTIAN WITNESS

1. Karl Barth, *The Word of God and the Word of Man,* trans. Douglas Horton (N.Y., Harper & Row, 1957), p. 16.
2. John Calvin, *Institutes,* Bk. II, Chap. II, 18, p. 299.
3. Martin Luther, *Luther's Works,* Vol. 22, ed. J. Pelikan (St. Louis, Concordia Publishing House, 1957), p. 51.
4. Barth goes too far when he asserts: "Preaching does not reflect, reason, dispute, or academically instruct. It proclaims, summons, invites, and commands." *Church Dogmatics,* IV, 3, b, trans. G. W. Bromiley (Edinburgh, T. & T. Clark, 1962), p. 869.

5. The liberal apologetic theologian, D. C. Macintosh, has written that it is the merit of the older apologetics that "it sought to advance reasons for the faith to which the unprejudiced and reasonable outsider *would have to yield his assent. . . .* " (Italics mine.) Douglas Clyde Macintosh, *The Reasonableness of Christianity* (N.Y., Charles Scribner's Sons, 1925), p. 2.
6. See esp. Howard Moody, "Toward a Religionless Church for a Secular World" in Stephen C. Rose, ed., *Who's Killing the Church?* (New York, Association Press, 1966), pp. 82-92.
7. See Clinton D. Morrison, *The Powers That Be* (Naperville, Alec R. Allenson, 1960).
8. See esp. Colin Williams, *Where in the World?* and *What in the World?* (N.Y., National Council of Churches, 1963 and 1964).
9. Dietrich Bonhoeffer, *No Rusty Swords,* trans. Edwin H. Robertson and John Bowden (N.Y., Harper & Row, 1965), p. 310.
10. A good example of a permanently valid insight in secular philosophy is Immanuel Kant's theory of radical evil propounded in his *Religion Within the Limits of Reason Alone* (N.Y., Harper & Row, 1960). Kant envisaged an evil innate in human nature which corrupts the ground of all moral maxims and is inextirpable by human powers. Yet this theory did not fit into his philosophical system and it was even set aside in this same work. Kant could not bring himself to abandon the optimism of the Enlightenment: "For man, therefore, who despite a corrupted heart yet possesses a good will, there remains hope of return to the good from which he has strayed" (p. 39).
11. Karl Barth, *Against the Stream,* ed. Ronald Gregor Smith (London, SCM Press Ltd., 1954), pp. 228, 229.
12. P. T. Forsyth, *The Principle of Authority* (London, Independent Press Ltd., 1952) 2nd ed., p. 33.
13. I seek to lay a theological basis for a theology of devotion in my books *The Christian Life and Salvation.* (Grand Rapids, Eerdmans, 1967), and *The Crisis of Piety* (Grand Rapids, Eerdmans, 1968).

Index of Subjects

Index of Names